THANK YOU FOR ATTENDING IN THE WILD VBS 2019 AT PENNWAY CHURCH OF GOD!

~ Pastor Becky & the Pennway Children's Ministry

ZOOM IN!
FOCUS ON
JESUS!

EXPLORE the BIBLE
DEVOTIONAL
A Book-by-Book Journey

written by Traci Perry

B&H
PUBLISHING GROUP
Nashville, Tennessee

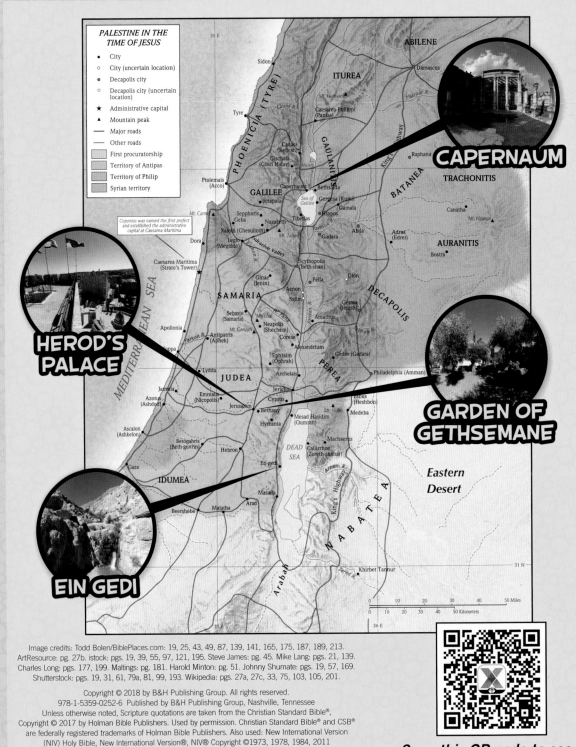

PALESTINE IN THE TIME OF JESUS

Legend:
- City
- City (uncertain location)
- Decapolis city
- Decapolis city (uncertain location)
- ★ Administrative capital
- ▲ Mountain peak
- — Major roads
- — Other roads
- First procuratorship
- Territory of Antipas
- Territory of Philip
- Syrian territory

Coponius was named the first prefect and established the administrative capital at Caesarea Maritima

CAPERNAUM

HEROD'S PALACE

GARDEN OF GETHSEMANE

EIN GEDI

Map labels: Abilene, Damascus, Iturea, Mt. Hermon, Sidon, Caesarea-Philippi (Panias), Raphana, Trachonitis, Litani R., Gaulanitis, Pharpar R., Batanea, Tyre, Phoenicia (Tyre), King's Highway, Cadesa (Kedesh), Gischala (Gush Halav), Huleh L., Canatha, Mt. Hauran, Ptolemais (Acco), Galilee, Capernaum, Bethsaida, Jotapata, Sea of Galilee, Gergesa (Kursi), Sepphoris, Geba, Nazareth, Tiberias, Hippos, Gamala, Auranitis, Xaloth (Chesulloth), Mt. Tabor, Gadara, Abila, Adraa (Edrei), Bostra, Dora, Legio (Megiddo), Jezreel Valley, Jordan R., Scythopolis (Beth-shan), Caesarea Maritima (Strato's Tower), Ginae (Jenin), Pella, Dion, Decapolis, Samaria, Aenon, Salim, Gerasa (Jerash), Apollonia, Sebaste (Samaria), Mt. Ebal, Neapolis (Shechem), Mt. Gerizim, Amathus, Antipatris (Aphek), Yarkon R., Coreae, Joppa, Alexandrium, Ephraim (Ophrah), Gedor (Gadara), Perea, Lydda, Judea, Archelais, Philadelphia (Amman), Jamnia, Emmaus (Nicopolis), Jericho, Cypros, Azotus (Ashdod), Jerusalem, Bethany, Mesad Hasidim (Qumran), Esbus (Heshbon), Hyrcania, Medeba, Ascalon (Ashkelon), Mt. Nebo, Betogabris (Beth-guvrin), Dead Sea, Callirrhoe (Zereth-shahar), Machaerus, Hebron, En-gedi, Eastern Desert, Gaza, Idumea, Masada, Arabah, Arnon R., Nabatea, Beersheba, Malatha, Arad, King's Highway, Zered R., Khirbet Tannur, Mediterranean Sea, Mt. Carmel, Salim, Jabbok R.

Scale: 0 10 20 30 40 50 Miles / 0 10 20 30 40 50 Kilometers

Copyright © 2018 by B&H Publishing Group. All rights reserved.
978-1-5359-0252-6 Published by B&H Publishing Group, Nashville, Tennessee
Unless otherwise noted, Scripture quotations are taken from the Christian Standard Bible®,
Copyright © 2017 by Holman Bible Publishers. Used by permission. Christian Standard Bible® and CSB®
are federally registered trademarks of Holman Bible Publishers. Also used: New International Version
(NIV) Holy Bible, New International Version®, NIV® Copyright ©1973, 1978, 1984, 2011
by Biblica, Inc.® Used by permission. All rights reserved worldwide.

DEWEY: C242.5 SUBHD: BIBLE--STUDY AND TEACHING \ DEVOTIONAL LITERATURE

Printed in Shenzhen, Guangdong, China in May 2018
1 2 3 4 5 6 • 22 21 20 19 18

Scan this QR code to see a digital version of the map with more VR experiences!

EXPLORE THE BIBLE!

HELLO PARENTS,

Thanks for choosing this resource to help build valuable Bible skills and increase biblical literacy for your kids. *Explore the Bible* is a resource that guides boys and girls book by book through the Scriptures. You may wonder why the books are arranged in the manner you see here, which might not seem to follow any real pattern. In reality, we are trying to introduce kids to the different types of literature they will encounter when they read their Bibles.

Divisions or *genres* are common words people use when talking about the way the Bible is structured. We have identified six different genres or types of writing found in the Bible. Law books give God's instructions for holy living. History books identify the history of God's people and how they interacted with Him and other nations. Prophecy books tell of things to come for the people at the time the book was written and beyond. Poetry and Wisdom books highlight the beauty of God's Word through poetic structure.

Gospel books share the good news of Jesus and His life, ministry, and sacrifice for sin. The Letters were written to individuals and churches to encourage and teach faithfulness to God and right living. The order of books in this resource gives a mix of genres while also introducing both Old and New Testament books on the same topic or theme. This structure will guide boys and girls to understand how each type of literature highlights God's message to His people.

To take the exploration even further, you can scan the QR code on the previous page to see several 360° virtual-reality videos of real places in the Holy Land. Check back often to see new videos.

It is our hope and desire that this resource gives your girls and boys a greater understanding of God's Word and a true desire to know Him better.

God bless!

CONTENTS

BOOKS OF THE BIBLE SUMMARIES Page 5

BIBLE SKILLS Page 218

DEVOTIONS Page 19

PARENT CONNECTION Page 224

BOOKS OF THE BIBLE SUMMARIES

THE LAW

These books begin with God's creation of the world and everything in it. They also tell about how sin came into the world when people broke God's law. But God promised to send a Savior to make everything right.

GENESIS

The book of Genesis is about our beginning. It tells of God forming the world and giving life. There is no creation without the Creator. Our existence proves His authority and supremacy. Genesis reveals God's power, patience, and provision through the story of His promise of salvation to an undeserving creation. God did not simply create us and turn away. He cares for His creation. He loves us. Even when we reject Him, He remains faithful. The book of Genesis is more than simply the story of the beginning of our existence. It is also the beginning of our redemption story.

EXODUS

God's promises are always fulfilled. The book of Exodus shows God unfolding the details of His plan that had been promised many years earlier. The Israelites were God's people who had been under strict oppression. Exodus details the journey of the Israelites as they escaped slavery and traveled to a promised land. However, it is more than a story of freedom. It reveals God's patience and faithfulness, and His willingness to dwell among His people.

The rebellion of the Israelites was constantly met with God's forgiveness. Although the people were accountable for their behavior, even their disobedience could not interfere with His sovereign plan.

LEVITICUS

The book of Leviticus can be summarized as holy instruction. This book emphasizes ceremonial practices intrinsic to the culture of the Israelites. Ritual sacrifices were a common topic because they represented the price of sin and purification. Such rituals no longer apply today, but the importance of holiness remains. The book of Leviticus repeatedly urges people to be holy. However, it is not a prompting to acquire holiness. It is an exhortation to reflect and honor God's holiness. Because God is set apart by His perfection, the command to be holy is an instruction to live a life set apart for Him.

NUMBERS

The book of Numbers depicts a transition between those Israelites who had participated in the exodus from Egypt and the next generation who would take possession of the promised land. The Israelites' repetitive complaints and disobedience did not deter God's faithfulness to fulfill His covenant. However, as God warned, rebellion had a severe impact; only two members of the original group were allowed to enter the land. We know from this book that our sovereign God does what He says He will do.

DEUTERONOMY

The book of Deuteronomy is filled with the final speeches Moses gave to the Israelites. He recounted their history of rebellion and consequences as well as their repentance and deliverance. He reminded them of God's faithfulness and mercy. With the Lord's commands, he challenged the next generation of Israelites to learn from previous mistakes and obey the Lord wholeheartedly. The last few chapters transition from the leadership of Moses to his successor, Joshua. At the close of the book, Moses was allowed by God to see the land of Canaan from a distance before his death.

OLD TESTAMENT HISTORY

The twelve books of history in the Old Testament contain some of the most exciting stories in all of the Bible, with some of the most amazing heroes.

JOSHUA

The main point of the book of Joshua is that we can trust God to keep His promises. The book begins with Joshua taking over after the death of Moses. The Israelites traveled with Joshua and participated in a series of interventions from God that included a dry path through the Jordan River, a crumbled city wall, a day the sun stood still, and so much more. This book explains the allotment of land that had been promised long before to Abraham. God's guidance and authority is evident throughout their journey, which is an encouragement to be faithful as God is faithful.

JUDGES

The book of Judges immediately follows the period of time when the Israelites had begun to take possession of the land God had promised. Although they had experienced God's miraculous provision and faithfulness, they wavered in their commitment to Him. Because of their disobedience, God allowed them to experience the influences and threats of other nations. However, He never abandoned them. Because of the book of Judges, we know that God's faithfulness and grace do not depend on our behavior. Sinful choices will always have consequences for us, but they will never change who God is.

RUTH

The book of Ruth describes a story that illustrates the inclusion of everyone in God's sovereign plan. When Ruth's husband died, she committed to remain with her mother-in-law. That decision, along with others that seemed insignificant at the time, proved to be an important step in God's larger plan. The book of Ruth shows that God's providence was not limited to Jewish men. Ruth was an ordinary Moabite woman used by God to unfold a series of events in history, and her name was recorded in Jesus' genealogy. We can trust God's plan in our lives. God does extraordinary things with ordinary circumstances.

1 SAMUEL

Israel was not always a nation led by a king. First Samuel describes the transition of Israel from being governed by judges to being a monarchy. The people of Israel wanted a king to rule over them.

Although the prophet Samuel warned of the consequences, they insisted. Unfortunately, Samuel's predictions proved to be true, and Israel's first king, Saul, did not obey God. The Lord replaced him with David, who understood that God is always truly in charge and even a king is accountable to Him. First Samuel teaches us that we cannot separate ourselves from God's authority.

2 SAMUEL

The book of 2 Samuel is a continuation of 1 Samuel. In fact, they were originally one book chronicling the establishment of a kingship in Israel. The foundation of 2 Samuel is God's covenant and deliverance experienced through the reign of David. It is essentially the history of David's rise, successes, and failures as king. Although the impact of sin is significant in 2 Samuel, David's flaws did not prevent God from using him to guide the Israelites away from idolatry. God's sovereignty is evident in 2 Samuel. God can always be trusted to maintain control and accomplish His plan.

1 KINGS

God warned the people of Israel many times after their rescue from Egypt that if they continued to rebel there would be consequences, and there were. Over and over the Israelites were subjected to unworthy kings. The author of the book of 1 Kings wanted to remind the people of their history. He tried to make it clear why they were in exile. The lessons of history revealed the consequences for their rebellion, but there was hope for mercy through repentance.

2 KINGS

The book of 2 Kings was originally part of 1 Kings. Therefore, it is best to consider the message and content as all one book. In the author's attempt to explain Israel's need to repent, the history of the divided kingdom and Babylonian captivity is recounted. The pattern of the nation and kings rising and falling together had not been enough to deter the Israelites from rebellion. Their exile and captivity fulfilled God's warnings of impending punishment. Second Kings points to the one true God who deserves undivided worship.

1 CHRONICLES

The book of 1 Chronicles is recognized for its connection with, and what some people consider dependence on, 1 and 2 Samuel as well as 1 and 2 Kings. In fact, some have suggested that it is impossible to fully understand the books independent of one another. It is believed that they were either sources of information for the writer of 1 Chronicles or that they used the same sources. The book emphasizes God's hand guiding human history to fulfill His sovereign plan of redemption.

2 CHRONICLES

As with 1 Chronicles, the book of 2 Chronicles is closely linked to 1 and 2 Samuel as well as 1 and 2 Kings. Second Chronicles was written to highlight the importance God placed on obedience to Him. Israel became a divided nation following Solomon's death. The nation divided continued its sin and eventually the people were taken into captivity by the Babylonians. Through this book we see God's patience, mercy, and faithfulness.

EZRA

The book of Ezra tells of the return of the exiles to Jerusalem and illustrates God's faithfulness and mercy. God had always promised restoration, even before the city fell, but this restoration was only a glimpse of what was to come later through Christ. Ezra taught the people and helped the people recognize their sin. Ezra began with a similar pattern of falling into sin, but this time the people repented.

NEHEMIAH

Nehemiah was a cupbearer for the king of Persia, Artaxerxes. He asked the king to allow him to go to Jerusalem to help rebuild the city. When Nehemiah arrived, he discovered that things were worse than he expected. The wall surrounding Jerusalem needed to be rebuilt. The people joined the effort and worked together in families to rebuild the wall. Because of the threats that came as they made progress, they worked with swords ready. Despite embarking on what might have seemed impossible in the beginning, Nehemiah's efforts were successful. It took only fifty-two days to completely rebuild the wall around Jerusalem.

ESTHER

The book of Esther shows God's sovereignty without specifically mentioning Him by name. It is a story of a woman named Esther who was selected to be the queen of Persia. She was faced with a dilemma of whether or not to make a request of the king. If he granted her request, it would save the Jews. The story provides an example of how it can look when God sovereignly accomplishes His will. The people involved were ordinary people making ordinary decisions. Through them, God protected the Jewish people and maintained His covenant.

WISDOM AND POETRY

The books of wisdom and poetry share wise sayings that help people live lives that are pleasing to God. Some of these books are written as poetry.

JOB

The primary theme of the book of Job is that God is sovereign and can be trusted. The book begins with Satan accusing a man named Job of insincere dedication to the Lord. God allowed Satan to test Job, which resulted in the destruction of Job's health, wealth, and children. Most of the book describes the turmoil of Job's struggle, and ends with a humble and repentant Job affirming God's sovereign plan before Job is restored.

PSALMS

The book of Psalms is a call to worship the divine Creator, Redeemer, and King. It is sometimes considered a collection of hymns, but might be better described as a book of praises. God is exalted in Psalms. The book is a genuine expression of the need for God and a tribute to His sovereignty. It includes honest pleas and complaints as well as triumphs and joy.

PROVERBS

The primary theme of the book of Proverbs is wisdom. The fear of the Lord and knowledge of God's Word, which are somewhat dependent upon one another, are also emphasized. Proverbs is filled with advice that contrasts the benefits of wisdom against the trouble of foolishness. Verses in Proverbs can be organized in a variety of ways to study or meditate on specific topics, relationships, doctrines, and more. Although it is typically thought of as a practical list, we can learn a lot about God through a close examination of the book of Proverbs.

ECCLESIASTES

According to the book of Ecclesiastes, everything the world has to offer is worthless. The author, who identified himself as the preacher or teacher, is believed to be the wise king Solomon. Solomon's conclusion was based on a thorough comparison of all possible accomplishments and the reality of death. Simply put, he concluded that nothing lasts. Everything in life is temporary and has no lingering purpose. Of course, that is not the only aspect of Solomon's assessment. He made sure to point out that this is only true without God. The Lord gives life meaning and makes all things worthwhile. His conclusion: live for God.

SONG OF SONGS

Love is the central focus of the book of Song of Songs. Some have attributed various symbolic meanings to the text, but it is generally accepted as poetic without underlying allegories. In other words, it is simply a book about love. God is love, and He relates to us in loving ways. God has given us the book of Song of Songs to help us understand love better, which will in turn help us understand Him better.

MAJOR PROPHETS

The books of prophecy tell the story of God's messages of hope and warning that were delivered by prophets over several hundred years. The five longest books of Prophecy are called major prophets.

ISAIAH

The book of Isaiah describes the way God used the prophet Isaiah to provide messages to His people. Isaiah's task was difficult because the messages he was required to share were not things the people wanted to hear. He warned people of God's judgment and explained the consequences of their disloyalty to God. They were warnings of condemnation to show that God would judge their sin. However, as with all of God's messages, there was hope. Isaiah reaffirmed God's promise to retain a remnant of Israel and offered hope to all of us through his prophesies about the Messiah.

JEREMIAH

The Israelites had ignored God's commands to repent long enough. It was time for God's judgment. In relaying this message, the prophet Jeremiah faced heavy opposition. He was constantly challenged for warning of the coming judgment. The people did not take his message seriously, and instead preferred predictions of prosperity and peace. Their idolatry continued as Jeremiah wept. Compared to the other biblical accounts of God's prophets, the book of Jeremiah depicts a more personal record of what it was like for a prophet to Israel. Jeremiah was badly mistreated but faithfully continued to spread God's message.

LAMENTATIONS

The book of Lamentations describes the anguish over the fall of Jerusalem. The Israelites had been disobedient and idolatrous for so long that they exhausted the opportunity God gave them to repent. The consequences included a series of evil rulers and defeats before the Israelites were eventually taken into captivity. The book of Lamentations is believed to have been written by Jeremiah. He had warned of the coming judgment, but the people continued their idolatry. Even after facing harsh treatment by the Israelites, Jeremiah grieved for them. This book depicts his heartbreak over the punishment that destroyed Jerusalem.

EZEKIEL

The book of Ezekiel is a straightforward message wrapped in poetic and symbolic prophecy. The core focus of the book is judgment against Israel and the other nations, then mercy to Israel. This book is full of unusual details of the prophet Ezekiel's experiences, such as eating a scroll, lying on his side for a year, and prophesying over dry bones. The unusual events and symbolic language balance the situation with Israel at the time, future restoration through Christ, and events still ahead of us.

MINOR PROPHETS

The books of prophecy tell the story of God's messages of hope and warning that were delivered by prophets over several hundred years. The twelve shortest books of prophecy are called minor prophets.

DANIEL

The book of Daniel weaves together history with prophecy. It is a collection of events connected less by chronology and more by God's sovereignty. It is specifically designed to show God's authority over the nations and how He is able to accomplish His will through individuals and groups. This book was written during the Babylonian exile to encourage the Jewish people with God's authority and plan. It remains an encouragement today for that very same reason.

HOSEA

The book of Hosea illustrates the repeated unfaithfulness of Israel and God's faithfulness through the troubled marriage of Hosea and Gomer. This graphic prophecy was another warning of coming judgement for Israel. God used Hosea to remind the Israelites of their rescue from Egypt and His provisions throughout the generations. The Israelites were also reminded of their many sins. Most importantly, though, they were reminded of God Himself. He deserved to be worshiped. Not only that, but whether He applied judgment or mercy, He was faithful to rescue and protect His people, even if He had to rescue them from their own rebellion.

JOEL

The book of Joel is poetic prophecy that warns of God's judgment. Although it is directed at Judah and Israel, it includes all humanity and the world. The book begins by describing a locust plague that is both literal and symbolic in meaning. The prophecy shows the absolute dependence all people have on God. The book of Joel is not simply a warning of impending destruction; it is an urgent call to repentance. Joel specifically emphasizes the Day of the Lord, which might be described as the full unveiling of God's power and judgment, thus the call to repentance.

AMOS

The language in the book of Amos is poetic, but the message is not pretty. Israel listened as Amos offered prophecies of coming judgment against neighboring enemies. The people were probably eager to hear the prophecies until Amos boldly announced the impending punishment of Israel. They had been simultaneously following the rituals of God's law while also engaging in idolatry and violence. God warned of destruction and exile, but it was not without hope. Because of His faithfulness, this judgment was part of His plan to turn the people back to Him so that Israel would eventually be restored.

OBADIAH

The book of Obadiah is a warning to Edom, but the history leading to this warning started in the book of Genesis. Jacob and Esau were twin brothers whose rivalry began in the womb. Their struggle against each other laid the foundation for contention between two nations: Edom and Israel. In one particular instance, the Edomites refused to allow the Israelites to cross their land. Another time they took part in a military assault on Jerusalem. Regardless of their aggression, God instructed Israel not to treat the Edomites the same way. Obadiah warned that Edom would not survive God's judgment.

JONAH

The book of Jonah is an illustration of God's sovereignty. It is the story of Jonah's resistance to share God's message of repentance with the people of Nineveh. Because Nineveh was an enemy of Israel, Jonah ran from this task. God caused him to be thrown into the sea, swallowed by a big fish, and vomited onto dry land. Despite Jonah's original resistance, God's message was delivered, and the people of Nineveh repented. Jonah represented the rebellion of Israel. God's authority over all things is evident throughout the book.

MICAH

Many have noticed the similarities in the messages of Micah and Isaiah. Some believe that because they both prophesied in Judah, Isaiah simply expanded on Micah's message. It is more likely that God gave them both similar messages. The Israelites had incorporated false religious practices into their worship of God. Micah was tasked with warning them to turn to God alone in worship or risk being destroyed. As serious as the messages were, they also included the hope of salvation. Micah even prophesied the birth of Jesus!

NAHUM

The book of Nahum depicts the unfortunate outcome for the city of Nineveh. This capital city of Assyria had been the destination many years earlier for the prophet Jonah. He watched in anger as God decided not to destroy Nineveh. Even though they believed Jonah's warning and cried out to God in repentance, they ultimately returned to their ruthless and violent ways. It was over a century later when Nahum warned of their impending destruction. This time God would not relent. Even though the destruction of Nineveh illustrates God's righteous judgment, it also shows His sovereign protection of Israel.

HABAKKUK

The book of Habakkuk reveals a lesson for all of us to learn. God does not need to earn worship; He deserves it because He is God. The prophet Habakkuk was frustrated with the people he was sent to preach to. He saw their rampant rebellion and wanted God to do something about it. Habakuk could not understand how blatant sin could go unpunished. He misunderstood God's larger plan and expected to see immediate results. His struggle led to a deeper and more joyful understanding of God's sovereignty and righteousness.

ZEPHANIAH

The book of Zephaniah is, like all the books of the twelve minor prophets, named for its author. Zephaniah prophesied during King Josiah's reign, who had attempted reform after the book of the Law was found after having been lost for many years. Zephaniah warned Judah of the Day of the Lord, a day coming when God would judge their sin.

Zephaniah is a picture of a broader warning to all of us. Zephaniah gives us an opportunity to turn to God from blatant rebellion before God sends judgment. God gives plenty of warning that now is the time to repent. Zephaniah's message was obviously not just for Judah.

HAGGAI

The book of Haggai is a lesson in priorities. The Israelites were allowed to return to Jerusalem after their captivity in Babylon. Although the rebuilding of the temple was to be their first priority when they returned, they quickly turned their attentions to lower priorities. They rebuilt other things and focused on homes for themselves. Because the efforts to rebuild the temple stalled, the people lived there many years without completing it. God sent Haggai to refocus their attention. The people remembered that God deserved honor and praise, and they repented. Once they were focused on God, He blessed them, and they saw Him do mighty things.

ZECHARIAH

When the Israelites were freed from Babylon to return to Jerusalem, they began rebuilding the temple. Discouragement from their neighbors interfered with the project. The people were less interested in building the temple than they were in their own homes and lives. Zechariah was sent to remind the people of their highest priority—God. Israel was challenged by Zechariah to repent and dedicate themselves to God. The call to repentance and worship extends to everyone.

MALACHI

Although the Israelites had been allowed

to return to Jerusalem from their captivity in Babylon, they struggled to continue worshiping God. They had opportunities to repent, but each time their repentance only lasted a little while. Within one hundred years of their return, they were more rebellious than at any other point in history. The prophet Malachi was sent to give them a message of coming judgment for all their grievous sins. Malachi's message was more than a warning; it also included a promise. Another messenger would come to prepare the way for redemption. That promised messenger was John the Baptist.

GOSPELS

The gospels tell the story of Jesus' birth, life, death, and resurrection. Each one tells the story of Jesus from a different perspective.

MATTHEW

The book of Matthew helps link the Old Testament promises of the coming kingdom to the New Testament fulfillment through Jesus. Jesus came to reveal His kingdom of righteousness and redemption. He reigns over all things and has authority to save sinners. Matthew identifies Jesus as the fulfillment of Old Testament prophecies and helps show His impact on the world as the fulfillment of God's covenant. Jesus is the promised one.

MARK

In a broad sense, the book of Mark might simply be described as a presentation of Jesus and His mission to save. More specifically, Mark focuses on Jesus as the suffering servant. His deeds, emotions, and self-applied limitations are on full display as His humanity is revealed throughout this book. Vivid descriptions of various encounters allow readers to feel almost as though they are experiencing the events themselves. Each chapter is filled with captivating tales of Jesus' life and ministry.

LUKE

The book of Luke focuses on the historical record of the life and ministry of Jesus to reveal salvation as His purpose on earth. This book provides a thorough description of the nativity story and describes the birth of John the Baptist. The book of Luke relates the personal nature of salvation. Luke emphasizes Jesus' compassion for those who are overlooked or rejected by society. Not only does this show that people from all backgrounds are loved by God and included in salvation, but it also helps illustrate the desperate need we have for God and His unmerited favor.

JOHN

Although the book of John includes teachings of Jesus not found in the other gospels, there is one primary theme—Jesus is the Christ, the Son of God. Not only does this book show the identity of Christ, but it also gives a full picture of what true Christianity entails. It is helpful to new believers or those who do not know Jesus because it offers basic but thorough knowledge of salvation and faith. John includes more detailed accounts of Jesus' teachings than Matthew, Mark, and Luke to thread the message of salvation throughout the book.

NEW TESTAMENT HISTORY

The book of Acts is the only book of history in the New Testament. The book is called Acts because it tells about the things the earliest followers of Jesus did through the help of the Holy Spirit. Acts tells the history of the early church.

ACTS

The book of Acts describes the establishment of the early church. We can see what it was like for those believers to begin to understand the changes that resulted from the death and resurrection of Jesus. Not only was everyone's understanding of salvation transformed, but the old cultural and legalistic ways were replaced. The gospel, which is the message of salvation through Jesus, was carried to people and places no one could have anticipated. The spreading of the gospel laid the foundation for redemption to be offered to people of every nation and background throughout every generation.

PAUL'S LETTERS

Paul was a missionary to many churches. He wrote thirteen letters to churches and individuals to give encouragement and to help them know how to live in ways that honor God.

ROMANS

There are so many important truths in the book of Romans that it has been described as the key to understanding the entire Bible. Although Romans explores several aspects of the Christian experience, the primary emphasis is that righteousness comes from God alone. It is essentially the comprehensive explanation of the gospel of Jesus Christ. The book of Romans includes theological teachings as well as practical instructions to fully illustrate God's justification of sinners by grace through faith in Christ. Through this book we can gain a thorough understanding of salvation and the righteousness that comes through the Savior.

1 CORINTHIANS

Paul wrote the book of 1 Corinthians to give guidance to the church in Corinth. Paul cared very much about the struggles of this church he started. He addressed their questions and problems by instructing them on several topics, such as division among believers, immorality, marriage, and resurrection. First Corinthians was intended to inform and correct. Paul not only offered practical insight, he also pointed to the gospel as the answer. The gospel is not something to learn and remember only as a moment in time. It applies to all aspects of life.

2 CORINTHIANS

When Christians are discouraged or facing struggles, the book of 2 Corinthians can bring comfort. It was written to encourage the church at Corinth and remains an encouragement to all believers. We can be confident in Jesus and take comfort in His strength. Our suffering and sin can be turned over to God. The book of 2

Corinthians also warns that many people and circumstances can distract and discourage believers from their confidence in God.

GALATIANS
The book of Galatians has a very straightforward theme: justification by faith. Paul wrote this book to Galatian believers who were being confused by Judaizers, false teachers who claimed that Gentiles had to become Jewish and practice Jewish rituals before being considered Christians. Judaizers did not understand how God's grace applied to Gentiles. This was not merely a cultural misunderstanding; it was a distortion of truth. Judaizers taught that adherence to the law was a requirement for salvation. Paul helped explain that the law had no power to save. It merely pointed to the Savior.

EPHESIANS
The book of Ephesians primarily focuses on the gospel message and how to live in honor of the Savior. It is an encouraging reminder to Christians of their immeasurable blessings from God. Ephesians describes the church as the body of Christ, which believers serve through various roles according to their spiritual gifts. A repeated theme throughout the book of Ephesians is the mystery of salvation, specifically that salvation includes Gentiles, which makes all believers equal before God. This book reveals how the gospel impacts every part of a person's life and is inspiration to live worthy of God's design.

PHILIPPIANS
The book of Philippians is a joyful letter encouraging believers to be Christlike. It is full of practical help for those who are growing spiritually and identifying with Jesus. One memorable passage explains Christ's humility as a servant, then seamlessly acknowledges Him as the one who deserves to be exalted. Throughout the book of Philippians, the instruction is focused on living in ways that honor Christ. There is a consistent attitude of rejoicing in the privilege of living for God. This book is a great reminder of why we should live a life that honors God.

COLOSSIANS
Paul wrote the book of Colossians to combat a collection of false teachings that were gaining influence. At the root of the problem was the idea that Jesus was not God and His sacrifice was not enough for salvation. There was an expectation that various legalistic practices had to be followed and special knowledge outside of Scripture had to be obtained. Paul emphasized the deity of Christ, reconciliation, redemption, and being made new in Him.

1 THESSALONIANS
The book of 1 Thessalonians was written by Paul to commend the Thessalonian church for continuing in the faith even without his leadership. They were facing resistance, yet they stood firm. Paul did not promise that their struggles would ease; he simply encouraged them to continue living for God. His specific suggestions included discipleship, sound doctrine, and living moral lives. His letter also included inspiration for them to develop a healthy church by looking to the future—the promise of Jesus' return.

2 THESSALONIANS

The book of 2 Thessalonians follows the praise and encouragement of 1 Thessalonians with reassurance and a little exhortation. The people were continuing to face pressure through increasing persecution and were beginning to get confused. Paul addressed some false teachings about the return of Jesus and challenged the believers to keep from being idle. Although there is significant prophecy in this book, it is also very practical. We can turn to the book of 2 Thessalonians as a reminder to stand firm against resistance and false teachers, to pray for fellow believers, to stay alert, and to avoid laziness.

1 TIMOTHY

The book of 1 Timothy includes some practical guidance, warnings of false teachers, and an overview of salvation. However, the general purpose of the book seems to be more of an instruction manual for church organization. First Timothy offers advice for church leaders as well as expectations and qualifications. Although Paul did not include a significant amount of theological instruction, sound doctrine is emphasized, particularly in the teachings about salvation. Paul clearly identified what should be theological priorities. Because of his guidance, churches have a biblical reference for how to structure and manage the work of ministry.

2 TIMOTHY

The book of 2 Timothy emphasizes the roles of leadership in the church, particularly that of the teaching pastors. Paul wrote to Timothy as a guide to help him avoid weaknesses and stay focused on the gospel. Although it contains obvious instruction for pastors and teachers, many helpful truths apply to any reader who wants to avoid weakness and stay focused on the gospel. Second Timothy will inspire all Christians to prioritize Scripture and never lose sight of Jesus.

TITUS

The book of Titus consists of three short chapters. It is instructional for church organization, particularly elders and overseers. It also emphasizes important doctrines such as justification by grace and substitutionary atonement. In this letter to Titus, the subject of salvation is so prominent that it is very possible that Paul was encouraging evangelism. This would have been a helpful tool to equip Titus and any other fellow leaders and believers for such ministry. It applies the same way for modern readers. We can gain insight and inspiration to share the message of the Savior from this encouraging resource.

PHILEMON

The book of Philemon tells a story of an appeal for forgiveness through the experiences of a man named Onesimus. He was a slave who ran away from his master, Philemon, and hid in Rome. At some point he met Paul and became a Christian. Onesimus returned to Philemon to surrender himself. Paul sent this letter to appeal to Philemon to forgive Onesimus. Paul genuinely loved Onesimus as a friend and fellow believer, and presented him that way to Philemon. Paul clearly wanted Philemon to think of Onesimus as a brother in Christ.

HEBREWS

The book of Hebrews compares the aspects of the old covenant with its fulfillment under the new covenant. In other words, Hebrews shows how the law could not overcome sin. The people needed a Savior. Old covenant priests and sacrifices became unnecessary because of the perfect sacrifice of the High Priest, Jesus. Jesus provided the permanent solution for the problem of sin, and He gave believers direct access to God. The book of Hebrews also addresses some practical issues, such as avoiding apostasy, persevering in faith, and accepting discipline.

GENERAL LETTERS

Some of Jesus' followers became missionaries, preachers, and teachers. Letters written to churches and individuals from these men are called the general letters.

JAMES

The book of James is full of instruction for life. It echoes the practical instruction of Proverbs. James is not intended to provide a list of rules. Instead, it inspires general obedience to God's Word as a full expression of faith. In fact, the emphasis of James is that true faith will be demonstrated by Christian living. James warns that knowing the truths of Scripture is not enough. Truth must be lived. However, mere outward obedience is not a reflection of true faith either. Godly character must be the result of faith, and faith will result in godly behavior.

1 PETER

Throughout the book of 1 Peter, mistreated and displaced believers are encouraged to stand firm in their faith. Followers of Jesus were facing difficulties simply because of their faith. Those who align with Jesus will always encounter resistance. This book is a reminder of what an honor it is to live for Jesus—the one who suffered on behalf of sinners.

2 PETER

The book of 2 Peter is similar to 1 Peter because both encourage believers to stand firm in their faith. While 1 Peter emphasizes the importance of focusing on Jesus during difficult circumstances, 2 Peter warns against false teachings. God's truth is emphasized as the strongest defense against the appeal of such lies. Although there are only three chapters, this book is full of helpful guidance and knowledge. In fact, one of the most important statements about Jesus is found in the very first verse of 2 Peter, which is where Jesus is identified as God and Savior.

1 JOHN

The apostle John wrote the book of 1 John to ensure a proper understanding of basic Christianity. It was written to identify the truth about Jesus and to help the readers recognize false teachings. There was a need for believers to understand Christ's humanity, divinity, and authority to save. In addition to guiding believers away from false teachings, John emphasizes the importance of Christian joy and fellowship and gives assurance of salvation. First John is a loving reminder of who Jesus is and what it looks like to live for Him.

2 JOHN

The book of 2 John was written to address the same false teachings referred to in the book of 1 John. There was a need to protect the purity of the gospel message since it was being corrupted. There were intentional efforts to convert believers to a different understanding of the gospel. Because those who were corrupting the church took advantage of the believers' hospitality, it created confusion about how to interact. John focused his readers on continuing to walk in truth. This book explains that truth is a basic requirement of genuine fellowship with Christ and others.

3 JOHN

The book of 3 John was written as an encouragement to a man named Gaius.

Apparently some who would travel to preach were not treated with genuine hospitality by other believers. Gaius was commended for showing a level of hospitality that reflected true obedience to God. According to John, he was behaving in a manner worthy of God. The message of this letter is that when believers live according to God's Word, they are going to reflect selfless, hospitable, generous behaviors. That message is true for all expressions of Christian faith. John called it walking in truth.

JUDE

An apostate is someone who appears to live as a Christian then completely turns away from God. The book of Jude warns to pay attention and not be misled by such people. The impact of their influence can remain long after they are gone. This book urges us to learn the truth about Jesus and share it with others. Jude helps us see how accurate knowledge of Christ can hold us firmly in place when error and confusion threaten to pull us away from truth.

PROPHECY

Revelation is the only book of prophecy in the New Testament. Revelation is the last book in the Bible and was written by one of Jesus' disciples, John. John wrote down the things God told him about how Jesus will come back and make everything right again.

REVELATION

The book of Revelation is mostly prophetic and full of symbolism, but the most important subject of this book is Jesus. Much is included about Jesus that supports what is already revealed in the rest of Scripture, namely that He is the Savior. This concluding message of the Bible tells us that Jesus will return. He will gather God's people and eliminate sin from the world. The earth will be made new and perfect, and God's people will spend eternity with Him.

DEVOTIONS

GENESIS

OUR CREATOR IS FAITHFUL

TEXT TRUTH

God is faithful to be including people today in the promise He made to Abraham.

EXAMINE THE TEXT

GENESIS 1:1; 2:15–17; 3:6; 17:1–8

It is an adventure to read the book of Genesis because it shows us so much about God and what He has done for us. This book helps us know God better by describing what He did in the past and what He promised for the future. Every chapter shows more and more about Him. Even the very first verse, Genesis 1:1, tells us a lot about God's power and supremacy.

Supremacy means that God has more authority and higher status than anyone else. He is the Creator. All things exist because of Him, and all things are under His authority. God is in charge. Everything belongs to Him, and everyone is accountable to Him.

Sadly, people do not honor God the way He deserves to be honored. We can see in Genesis 2:15–17 and 3:6 that God gave a restriction to Adam, the man He created, but Adam did not do things God's way. We are all like Adam. We are all guilty of doing things our own way instead of God's way.

What are some things you have done your own way instead of God's way? How do you feel about those decisions? Even if something is fun for a little while, when it is not what God wants, it can make us sad later. If you love God, your sin will always bother you, because it always bothers God.

MEMORY VERSE

GENESIS 1:1

In the beginning God created the heavens and the earth.

ABRAM'S TENT

Thankfully, He is patient and forgiving.

In Genesis 17:1–8, God made a promise to an imperfect man named Abram. God offered Abram a blessing and a legacy that would last for eternity, and that showed God's faithfulness and forgiveness. He promised that Abraham would be blessed as the father of many nations, but it was for more than a large biological family. God's blessing was a promise that people throughout many generations would be adopted into God's family.

The good news is that God's eternal promise to Abraham is still available today. You can be part of God's family because the promise God made to Abraham is fulfilled through Jesus. His sacrifice on the cross made a way for sinners to be adopted into God's family. Jesus paid the price for sin so we can be forgiven.

Have you ever gone camping in a tent? Can you imagine living in one for many years? That's exactly what Abram did! God had a plan for Abram and Abram had faith in God and in His promises. As Abram's family trusted and followed God, they had to pack up and move from place to place many times. Living in tents allowed them to relocate and make a home wherever God led.

GENESIS

God created all things and has authority over all things. (Genesis 1:1).

God is perfect, but people are sinful (Genesis 3:6).

God is forgiving and faithful (Genesis 17:7).

Genesis 1:1 shows us that God rules, and we are accountable to Him. Since we are all sinners like Adam, we do not deserve to be a part of God's family. That is why His promise is so loving. Instead of punishment, He offers forgiveness to those who turn away from sin and trust in Jesus.

You can talk to God about His forgiveness and ask Him to help you understand what His promise to Abraham means for your life. Remember, you can be part of God's family through Jesus, because God is faithful to keep His promises and forgive sin.

PRAYER

Find a place without any distractions, and spend a few minutes talking to God. You do not have to use special words or phrases. It is as simple as having a conversation.

Thank God for all He created and the life He gave you. Thank Him for being forgiving and faithful. You can talk to Him about times you have done things your own way instead of His way, then ask Him to forgive you and help you become more faithful.

ACTS
THE GOSPEL CHANGES EVERYTHING

TEXT TRUTH

The message of Jesus is important enough to share with others even when it is difficult.

MEMORY VERSE

ACTS 9:20
Immediately he began proclaiming Jesus in the synagogues: "He is the Son of God."

EXAMINE THE TEXT

ACTS 7:59-8:3; 9:1-5, 20-23; 14:19-23

Have you ever been so excited about something that you could not wait to tell people? Maybe you were invited on a trip or given a pet. As you read the verses in Acts, you will notice that there was a message being shared, but it was not about pets or trips.

Today, many people live where it is not dangerous to trust Jesus, but others risk their safety to follow Him. The believers described in the book of Acts faced harsh treatment. One graphic example of that is described in Acts 7:59–8:3.

Stephen was stoned for preaching while Saul approved of his death and searched for other believers to punish. It must have been so scary for Stephen.

He had a message that he was excited to share, but those who heard it attacked him. To Stephen, it did not matter how they reacted. He kept speaking because he knew it was important to tell them about Jesus.

Talking about Jesus might not seem very dangerous, but the gospel message changes everything. When someone learns about Jesus, nothing is ever the same. Every person will either trust Him or reject Him. Some people will even try to keep others

ACTS

Stephen and Saul, also known as Paul, proclaimed Jesus even when they faced danger (Acts 7:60, 14:19-20).

Jesus turned Saul's life around (Acts 9:1, 20).

You can trust Jesus with your life.

You can share the powerful message of Jesus with others.

from hearing about Him. That is what Saul tried to do, but nothing can destroy the truth of Jesus.

Acts 9:1–5 shows that Saul was on a destructive mission, threatening disciples and looking for people to arrest, when he met the Savior. He looked at what others were doing instead of looking at his own sin. He thought he was right to try to destroy what threatened his religion. However, God did not approve. Fortunately for Saul, Jesus opened his eyes to the truth and gave him a new mission.

Saul began to stand for Jesus rather than against Him. In the first verse of chapter 9, Saul was threatening disciples, but by verse 23 he was the target of those same kinds of threats. He approved of Stephen's being stoned for preaching about Jesus, but Acts 14:19–23 tells us that he was later stoned for the same reason. Unlike Stephen, he survived and continued to preach the message of Jesus.

Saul, who was also known as Paul, would not be discouraged from his mission for Jesus. Although he faced many obstacles, he kept preaching and helped strengthen the believers as more joined them. Stephen and Paul are good examples of what it can look like to trust Jesus. Of course, not everyone will be in danger like they were, but trusting Jesus means living for Him no matter what we face.

Paul and Stephen were just two of the men who helped spread the message of Jesus. The church grew and believers continued to tell others about Jesus for many generations, and it is still growing today. We now know about Jesus because people were willing to risk their lives to share His message. You can trust Jesus and continue to share His message with others too.

ON THE ROAD TO DAMASCUS

On the way to Damascus, Saul's life was changed in an unexpected way when he met Jesus. Because of Saul's experience, many lives were changed. Saul became known as Paul, one of the greatest missionaries in the history of the church!

PRAYER

Many people risked their lives to share the message that Jesus died for us and that He rose from the grave. Thank God for His gift of salvation and that He made a way for you to know that Jesus died on a cross to pay for sin. Ask God for the same courage that the early believers had to follow Him and share His message.

1 SAMUEL

GOD REIGNS OVER ALL

TEXT TRUTH

We can never do anything to undo God's authority.

EXAMINE THE TEXT

1 SAMUEL 8:1–22

God is in control. It might not always seem that way, but He is. No one has more power than He does, no problem is too difficult for Him, and no one can get rid of Him. We can see in 1 Samuel 8:1–22 that even when people are arrogant and disobedient, God is still in control.

The story is very simple. The people of Israel were not happy with the priests and judges, so they asked for a king. Samuel attempted to discourage their request, but they kept demanding an earthly ruler, so God gave them what they asked for.

The idea of a king for Israel was not new. God's people had asked for a king many times. God had a plan, but the people of Israel insisted on being like the other nations. God had chosen Israel for a much greater role in His plan. Israel was never meant to be like other nations. They were selected to be set apart.

God knew the motives of the people. He knew they were rejecting Him. They did not want to be accountable to God, but what they did not understand was that their plan to appoint a king did not remove God's authority. Any king who would rule Israel would also be

MEMORY VERSE

1 SAMUEL 8:7

The LORD told him, "Listen to the people and everything they say to you. They have not rejected you; they have rejected me as their king."

Crowns have been a symbol of royalty and authority for thousands of years! Here are a few from around the world!

subject to God. No king would ever be able to take God's place. They could not get rid of God.

Even though the people of Israel were wrong to reject God, they thought they had good reasons to want things to change. The priests and judges had become corrupt. There were definitely problems that needed to be solved, but they did not want to depend on God for help. Instead, they wanted to do things their own way.

It is always better to depend on God than to depend on our own plans. Every person can probably relate to the people of Israel in some way.

1 SAMUEL

The request for a king was also a rejection of God (1 Samuel 8:7).

KEY POINTS

Even Israel's king would be under God's authority (1 Samuel 13:13-14).

God is always the final authority (1 Samuel 10:9).

It is tempting to get rid of problems on our own while also rejecting God's authority. It sometimes seems like it could make life easier to do things our own way, but it is never easier. It never solves the problems. It only replaces them with different ones.

Problems exist because people are sinners. As long as there are people in the world, there will be difficulties to face. Thankfully, God is not discouraged or distracted by people's choices. He does not lose His authority when people make bad decisions. We can learn from this example that there is no one who has more authority than God. No one can get rid of Him, and no one is more powerful. Even kings are accountable to Him. God is in control.

PRAYER

There are things in life that can be disappointing or difficult. You might have circumstances you would like to change, especially if there are people in your life who are negative influences and encourage you to sin. You can ask God to help you obey Him even when people around you are rejecting Him. You can trust God with your problems, because His solutions are always best.

MATTHEW
PRAY WITH THE RIGHT MOTIVE

TEXT TRUTH

Jesus tells us that our prayers should focus on honoring God, not impressing other people.

MEMORY VERSE

MATTHEW 6:9-13

"You should pray like this: Our Father in heaven, your name be honored as holy. Your kingdom come. Your will be done on earth as it is in heaven. Give us today our daily bread. And forgive us our debts, as we also have forgiven our debtors. And do not bring us into temptation, but deliver us from the evil one."

EXAMINE THE TEXT

MATTHEW 6:5-13

Sometimes prayer can be very similar to talking to a friend. You probably have someone in your life who makes you feel comfortable talking about things you enjoy or things you want. Maybe you have complimented your friend. It is possible you have even asked your friend to help you understand things that do not always make sense. None of those kinds of conversations are unusual. They are all ordinary ways to communicate with friends. They are also ordinary ways to communicate with God.

Prayer is like a conversation with God. Even though prayer can be similar to a regular conversation, if you have ever talked to God before, you already know that conversations with Him are different than they are with everyone else. When we pray, instead of speaking the words out loud,

KEY POINTS

We communicate with God through prayer (Matthew 6:6).

God communicates with us through the Bible and hearing from other people (2 Timothy 3:16).

Jesus told us to honor God and turn to Him for forgiveness (Matthew 6:9, 12).

we can think the words in our minds. We sometimes bow our heads and close our eyes to focus on God and show respect to Him. One of the biggest differences is that instead of hearing His voice, He talks to us through the Bible or through other people.

Jesus gives some instruction on prayer in Matthew 6:5–8. He warns about praying just to be seen by other people. Of course, praying out loud in front of others or with others can be very good. Jesus wants us to pray for the right reasons and not just to impress people or to feel important.

In the next few verses, Matthew 6:9–13, Jesus tells us some things to include in prayers. Jesus tells us to always honor God, because God is holy. Prayer also includes an element of seeking forgiveness for sin. Even if those things are not mentioned exactly the same way in every prayer, they are important to keep in mind.

When you think about your relationship with God, ask yourself if you honor God and understand your need for forgiveness. If not, you can ask God for help. In fact, you might want to make that your next prayer. Remember, we all sin, but God is holy, which means He is perfect. God requires payment for all our sins, but the good news is that Jesus died on the cross as a gift of love to pay the price for sin. You can turn from your sin and trust Jesus as your Savior and Lord. As you spend time talking to God today, be sure to read your Bible to see what He wants to say to you.

JESUS PRAYED

Jesus spent time praying to God. He knew that prayer was important. One place where He went to pray was the Garden of Gethsemane on the Mount of Olives. A church was later built there, but thousands of olive trees remain.

PRAYER

You might remember from Matthew 6:8 that God already knows your needs. As you talk to Him today, be honest about your feelings, your needs, and your thoughts. He will not be surprised by anything you tell Him. Remember that God is holy and deserves honor. Be sure to thank Him for His kindness in providing the Bible, teaching us how to pray, and forgiving sin.

1 PETER
SUFFER FOR JESUS AND WITH JESUS

TEXT TRUTH

We should honor Jesus when we face persecution and know we are never alone in our suffering.

EXAMINE THE TEXT

1 PETER 3:14-16

There are a lot of serious things to think about when we read the Bible. The topic in today's reading is one of those serious issues. It reminds us that being a Christian is not always easy. There are examples in the Bible of people who suffered quite a bit simply because they followed Jesus. Why do you think they were willing to suffer for Christ? Here is a hint: 1 Peter 3:14–16.

Persecution is when people are mistreated for being part of a group. Persecution is usually more dangerous than disagreements and much more serious than simply not liking someone. People are persecuted when they are targeted with intimidation or harm because of cultural, religious, or physical differences.

This is not easy to talk about. It would be nice not to have to think about such terrible things, but God wants us to know about this problem and to be ready to handle similar issues. Knowing what has happened to others will help us think of how much we care about God. It will cause us to ask ourselves if we would be willing to suffer for Him.

God does not want anyone to mistreat other people, so persecution is sin. Sadly, people do not always do things God's way.

MEMORY VERSE

1 PETER 3:14

Even if you should suffer for righteousness, you are blessed. Do not fear what they fear or be intimidated.

Christians are often described as the most persecuted group in the world. We have verses like 1 Peter 3:14–16 to prepare us for times when we might be mistreated. That is something useful to know, but according to verse 14, it is not something to fear. We might never be able to fully understand why people persecute others, but we know from this passage that believers who are persecuted have hope in Jesus. Suffering is temporary, but His blessing is eternal.

We can see in verses 15 and 16 that Christ deserves to be honored as holy. He is the reason for hope. We can set our minds on Him and determine to do what is right. That way we have no guilt, and others will see a difference in us.

The Colosseum was built in Rome almost 2,000 years ago. Christians were persecuted because of their faith in front of huge crowds gathered in this arena. Peter wrote to the persecuted Christians.

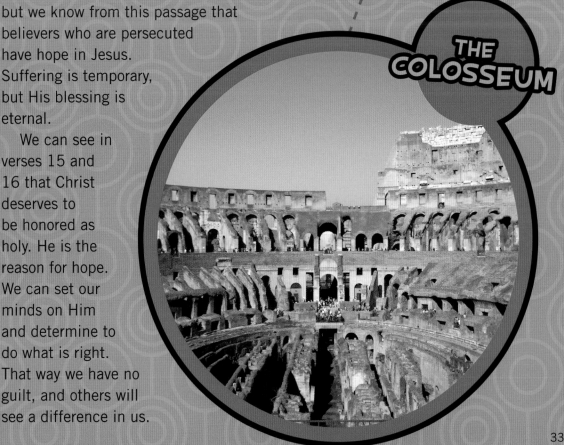

THE COLOSSEUM

1 PETER

KEY POINTS

Do not fear being persecuted (1 Peter 3:14).

Honor Jesus, even during persecution (1 Peter 3:15).

Be a good example to those who persecute you (1 Peter 3:16).

Be ready to tell others about Jesus (1 Peter 3:15).

Also, when others need to know about Jesus, we should be prepared to tell them, no matter how they treat us.

The Bible describes many examples of persecution because God wants us to be aware of suffering and know how to respond to mistreatment. Hopefully you will never see any persecution, but you can always honor God by focusing on Jesus, being a good example, and telling others of God's love.

PRAYER

Before praying, spend a little time thinking of your commitment to Jesus, and ask yourself if you are willing to suffer for Him. Pray for the knowledge and courage to respond the way God wants you to in every situation. If you have ever mistreated people or reacted the wrong way when people have mistreated you, you can ask God to help you apply what you learned from today's Bible verses to always honor Him.

2 PETER

BE EFFECTIVE AND FRUITFUL

TEXT TRUTH

God has given us everything we need to live productive lives for Him.

EXAMINE THE TEXT

2 PETER 1:3-8

The Bible tells us how to keep from being ineffective and unfruitful. You can see it for yourself in 2 Peter 1:8. If you are wondering what it means to be ineffective and unfruitful, it is basically a way to describe a person whose life does not produce any good results. No one wants to be ineffective and unfruitful, so it is terrific that God tells us exactly how to live productive lives. God wants more than accomplishments and positive results. He is giving us what we need to live lives that honor Him.

To live for God, there is something extremely important to know. We are all sinners. Some people think that it is possible to do good things in the world and that doing good makes up for the bad things. But sin is not erased by good deeds. No matter how many good choices you make, they will not repair the impact of sin. That is something only Jesus can do. God will punish every sin. He will not measure bad behavior against good behavior. That is why everyone needs Jesus. When Jesus died on the cross, He took the punishment for sin. His sacrifice makes it possible for us to be acceptable to God.

MEMORY VERSE

2 PETER 1:3
His divine power has given us everything required for life and godliness through the knowledge of him who called us by his own glory and goodness.

2 PETER

Christians can live a productive life that honors God (2 Peter 1:3-4).

Our choices cannot give us salvation, but they can make us effective and fruitful (2 Peter 1:8).

God wants us to live for Him (2 Peter 1:5-7).

We cannot behave well enough to earn forgiveness, but we can make fruitful choices—choices that honor God. Those who know God are free from sin. They are able to live for Him. Verses 5 through 7 tell us how. It might seem confusing, but it is actually very simple.

Writing down a few key words can help you see the main point of the verses. Begin with the word *faith*. Verse 5 tells us that there is something that should be added to or supplement your faith. Depending on the translation of the Bible you are using, that thing is goodness, virtue, or moral excellence. That is the next word or phrase you should write down. Look for other key words from these verses and write down those too. Your list will be similar to the following one: *faith*, *virtue*, *knowledge*, *self-control*, *steadfastness*, *godliness*, *brotherly affection*, *love*. Do these words describe your life? They describe the kind of life God wants for each of us. He encourages us to rely on Him to bring forth these qualities in our lives.

You already know why we would want to have these qualities. Verse 8 clearly tells us that these traits keep us from being ineffective and unfruitful. You might want to keep these words in a place where you can look at them often to remember the guidance of these verses. They tell you what you need to live a productive life for the Lord. You can live a life that honors God.

BE FRUITFUL

PRAYER

The Bible helps us understand God and how He wants us to live. The passage you read today gave specific guidance on how to live for the Lord. It is nice to have the Bible to help us honor God. You can thank the Lord for loving us enough to give us the Bible and for giving us everything we need to live fruitful lives. Ask Him to help you apply what you learned today.

To be fruitful is to show our love for Jesus in our actions. It is one of the characteristics of true obedience to God. Jesus talked about the importance of being fruitful. He described a tree that bore fruit as showing its usefulness, but He said that a tree that did not bear fruit needed to be cut down.

JUDE
STAY TRUE

TEXT TRUTH

If we focus on Jesus and the truth of the Bible, we will not be deceived by false messages.

EXAMINE THE TEXT

JUDE 1:17–21

The book of Jude is one of the shortest books in the Bible. Its title almost makes it seem like it should be one of the Old Testament books, but it is actually in the New Testament. It is the next-to-the-last book in the Bible, and depending on the notes and extra materials in your Bible, it is possible that the entire book is printed on a single page. The book of Jude is one of only a handful of books in the Bible that does not have chapters. When you read Jude, you can say that you read an entire book of the Bible!

This book was written by one of the half brothers of Jesus at a time when people who had been with Jesus were still sharing their testimonies. Those who had formed the church were excited about joining other believers to worship, but it was a vulnerable time because there was enormous threat to the church.

Many religious and political leaders were unhappy that so many people

MEMORY VERSE

JUDE 1:21

Keep yourselves in the love of God, waiting expectantly for the mercy of our Lord Jesus Christ for eternal life.

were still sharing the message of Jesus. They wanted to destroy that message, so they put a lot of pressure on the people who were following Christ. Jude warned that corruption was not only going to come from the obvious resistance they could see from the outside of the church, but it would also come from their fellowship within the church. When you read Jude 1:17–19, you will see that the warning of division was very serious. People joining in the activities of worship were introducing lies and distortions.

How do you know if something is untrue, and how do you avoid being deceived? The best way is to know what is true. We can depend on the Bible for that. Jude 1:20–21 helps us understand how to keep from being deceived. First, those verses tell us to trust Jesus. Get to know His message

THE TORAH

Jude warned believers that people would say wrong things about God and Jesus. In Old Testament times, when the Law was found and read, it changed the people of God. When we read the Word of God, it changes us and transforms us to be more like Him! The Law is called the Torah and Jews keep copies in synagogues in cases called arks.

JUDE

KEY POINTS

We can avoid deception by relying on faith in Christ, prayer, God's love, and the promise of eternal life (Jude 1:20–21).

Knowing God helps us recognize and stand firm against false teachings (Jude 1:24).

through Scripture, and rely on Him for truth. Genuine faith in Christ and proper understanding of His sacrifice guards against confusion. Second, they tell us to talk to God. Prayer is a tool that can keep us focused on the Lord and what He is doing in our lives. Third, these verses tell us to rest in the love of God. He is the source of truth, and His love can protect against any misconception. Fourth, they tell us to look to the future return of Jesus. The troubles of this life are temporary, but God offers eternal life. When we remember the big picture, we can see things more clearly.

At some point, everyone has believed something that was not true. It can be confusing, especially if the deception seems very close to the truth. Jude 1:20–21 tells us that we can rely on faith, prayer, the love of God, and the mercy of Christ to stay true as others are attempting to deceive us. Trust God and the truth of the Bible.

PRAYER

No one wants to be misled. If we apply what we learn from God's Word, we can be more prepared to recognize false teachings. Thank God for giving you truth through the Bible, and ask Him to help you live according to what you are learning. You can ask Him to help you know what is true and recognize anything untrue. Maybe take a minute to pray for anyone who is confused about God.

JOSHUA
WILL YOU OBEY AND SERVE THE LORD?

TEXT TRUTH

If we claim to love God, it should be evident in how we live.

EXAMINE THE TEXT

JOSHUA 24:22-24

Have you ever made a promise to someone? Maybe you agreed to complete a task or offered to help with something in the future. Were you able to keep your promise? Sometimes unexpected things can prevent us from keeping our commitments. Even though we sometimes fail to fulfill our promises, God never fails to fulfill His. His faithfulness can encourage us to do our best to live for Him and show our love for Him in every part of life.

When you read Joshua 24:22–24, you will see that Joshua is one of the few examples among the Israelites at the time who remained committed to God no matter what was happening. He encouraged faith in the Lord even while the people around him rebelled and complained. Joshua challenged his fellow Israelites to fulfill their commitment to serve and obey the Lord. Joshua told the Israelites to put away other gods. They were not concerned about God's role as the one and only true God.

It might not look the same today as it did for the Israelites, but other things are still being worshiped besides the only true God. You might notice people today worshiping things such as entertainment, comfort, or wealth. Other people literally worship false gods. Some even think there are

MEMORY VERSE

JOSHUA 24:24

The people said to Joshua, "We will worship the LORD our God and obey him."

41

JOSHUA

There is only one God (Joshua 24:23).

God deserves to be worshiped (Joshua 24:23).

Those who truly love God will serve and obey Him (Joshua 24:22-24).

many possible ways to get to heaven. Those are false beliefs and empty rewards. It is important to know that there is only one God. Only His grace offers forgiveness of sin and the promise of heaven. He is the only one worthy of worship.

Joshua reminded the Israelites that true commitment to God must be obvious in the way people live. He had previously warned them of God's righteous anger. By this point, they had begun to take his concerns more seriously. In verses 23 and 24, when Joshua gave the Israelites a chance to commit themselves to the Lord, they agreed to serve and obey God. That was a turning point for the Israelites. They had spent many years grumbling about life and complaining to God. Their experiences and hardships were no excuse to rebel or turn to false gods.

Even though the Israelites had seen the many wonderful and amazing things God did for them, they kept turning away from Him. Finally, with Joshua's guidance, they began to truly serve God. Those who genuinely love God will live for Him.

If you have ever claimed to love God, called yourself a Christian, or told others you were saved, then you have identified yourself as someone who is committed to the Lord. Everyone who makes that commitment should ask themselves if they live as people who love God. Worship only God and live for Him.

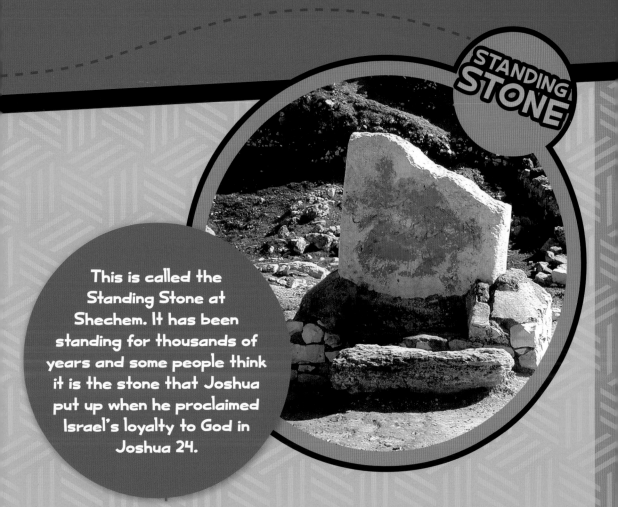

STANDING STONE

This is called the Standing Stone at Shechem. It has been standing for thousands of years and some people think it is the stone that Joshua put up when he proclaimed Israel's loyalty to God in Joshua 24.

PRAYER

Today's verses probably caused you to think about your commitment to God. Even if this is the very first time you have thought about God, you have the opportunity to serve and obey Him. Thank God for giving you the chance to recognize if you are worshiping anything other than Him. Talk to the Lord about anything you are putting ahead of Him. Ask God for help to serve and obey Him.

JUDGES

AROUND AND AROUND SIN GOES

TEXT TRUTH

If we follow God instead of our own standards, we can avoid a pattern of sin.

EXAMINE THE TEXT

JUDGES 17:6; 21:25

If you remember from the book of Joshua, the Israelites had finally stopped grumbling and rebelling. They turned to God and began to serve and obey Him. Unfortunately those Israelites did not prepare the generations that would follow to maintain that same obedience and reverence for God. The rebellion problems started again with a new generation of people who did not know God.

You can see in Judges 17:6 and 21:25 that there was no standard for how the people should live. Everyone just decided what they thought was right. Because there were different opinions and perspectives, there was no right or wrong. Imagine the problems that would cause!

MEMORY VERSE

JUDGES 21:25
In those days there was no king in Israel; everyone did whatever seemed right to him.

Who do you think decides whether something is right or wrong? The Bible tells us in the book of James that there is only one lawgiver and judge—God. He is the only one who has authority to determine right and wrong.

When the Israelites turned away from God, He withdrew His protection. Like so many years earlier, they were subject to oppression. They were vulnerable and weakened.

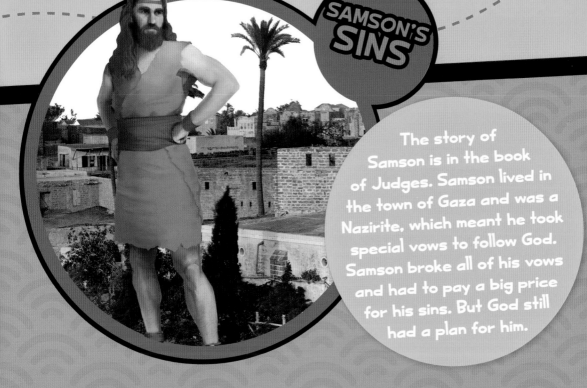

The story of Samson is in the book of Judges. Samson lived in the town of Gaza and was a Nazirite, which meant he took special vows to follow God. Samson broke all of his vows and had to pay a big price for his sins. But God still had a plan for him.

They were no longer the obedient Israelites of Joshua's time, but there was something familiar about what was happening. The book of Judges shows a repeating pattern: service, sin, consequences, repentance, and deliverance.

The Israelites kept repeating the same pattern. They would serve God, then sin. Their sin would cause terrible consequences, then they would cry out to God in repentance. God would forgive them and rescue them, then they would serve Him again.

It shows us what happens when people stop appreciating God, but it also shows His patience and forgiveness. Through this pattern in the book of

Judges, we can also see God's authority. God used different judges to repeatedly deliver the Israelites out of the hands of their enemies: Othniel (Judges 3:9–11); Ehud (Judges 3:12–30); Shamgar (Judges 3:31); Deborah (Judges 4–5); Gideon (Judges 6:11–8:35); Tola (Judges 10:1–2); Jair (Judges 10:3–5); Jephthah (Judges 11:1–12:7); Ibzan (Judges 12:8–10); Elon (Judges 12:11–12); Abdon (Judges 12:13–15); Samson (Judges 13–16).

As you read about all the different judges, you might notice that one man is missing from the list. His name was Abimelech (Judges 9). He established himself as the leader without officially gaining the authority as a judge.

JUDGES

God is the one who determines what is right and wrong (Judges 17:6).

The pattern the Israelites kept repeating shows us God's patience, forgiveness, and authority (Judges 2:1).

The judges were often very similar to military leaders. Abimelech took that role, but instead of guiding the Israelites out of trouble, he caused trouble. He seems to be another example of what can happen when people do what is right in their own eyes instead of relying on God for guidance.

We can learn from the Israelites' example and avoid a pattern of sin. Instead of deciding for ourselves, we can look to God for what is right or wrong. We do not have to repeat the same mistakes. We can trust authority and do things His way.

We can use the Israelites' example as a reminder to avoid returning to sin (Judges 2:13-14).

PRAYER

We can learn from the struggles the Israelites faced every time they turned to sin. You can talk to God about the struggles sin causes in your life. God is the only one who has authority to deliver us from sin. If you have not been following God, now is a good time to turn from sin and turn to Him. You can apologize for your sin, ask for forgiveness, and request that He help you avoid sin in the future.

RUTH
LITTLE THINGS CAN MAKE A BIG DIFFERENCE

TEXT TRUTH

When we follow God, we can know that we are always making the right decisions.

EXAMINE THE TEXT

RUTH 1:6-7, 15-16; 2:8-12

If you flip a coin over and over again, it will be impossible to predict which face it will land on. Even if you sometimes guess correctly, there will be no pattern because it is random.

MEMORY VERSE

RUTH 2:12

May the LORD reward you for what you have done, and may you receive a full reward from the LORD God of Israel, under whose wings you have come for refuge.

Sometimes life feels that way. It feels like everything is random and there is no way to know what to expect. The book of Ruth shows us that there is purpose in things that may sometimes seem random. Even when we do not know what will happen, we can trust God to lead us.

In the beginning of the book of Ruth, a famine drove a woman named Naomi to move to Moab with her husband and two sons. Sadly, her husband died, and she was left in Moab with her sons. Eventually her sons married Moabite women. Unfortunately, her sons also died, leaving Naomi with her daughters-in-law, Orpah and Ruth.

In Ruth 1:6–7, you will see that Naomi wanted to go back home when she heard the Lord had provided food. There were many things for her to consider, but her decision was based on God. Naomi kept her focus on the Lord, but she was not the only one. When Orpah and Ruth began to travel with her, she urged them to return to Moab.

RUTH

KEY POINTS

It is better to follow God than to make random decisions (Proverbs 3:5-6).

In Ruth 1:15–16, Orpah returned to her family and gods, but did you notice what Ruth did? She stayed with Naomi and committed to follow the one true God! At that time, women were not always treated well, and widows were especially vulnerable. Ruth faced a particular difficulty because she was going where Moabite women were not accepted. Instead of returning to her family or finding another husband for protection, she followed where God was leading.

Naomi and Ruth did not know where their decision would lead, but they relied on God to determine their steps. At first, it might have been frightening. They had very little, so Ruth gathered food from what was left in a field after the harvest. The field was owned by Boaz, a relative of Naomi's late husband. When Boaz discovered her in his fields, he was kind and generous. You can read Ruth 2:10–12 to see how he responded when asked about his generosity. Boaz recognized Ruth's sacrifices and wanted her to be rewarded. He offered her food and protection, and eventually they got married.

Ruth could not have known where her decisions would lead, but the Lord guided her and rescued her. We will not always be able to predict what will happen. We might even think that some decisions do not matter. But when we follow God, all our decisions will lead us to what He wants for our lives. We can trust God to guide us to whatever we need and whatever is best.

PRAYER

Ruth's most important decision was to stay focused on God. You can ask God to help you follow Him in all the choices you have to make. Any time you need help to know what God wants, you can ask Him to help you stay focused on what you are learning from the Bible.

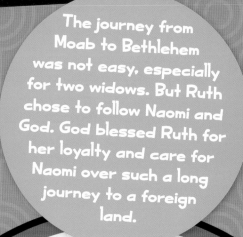

The journey from Moab to Bethlehem was not easy, especially for two widows. But Ruth chose to follow Naomi and God. God blessed Ruth for her loyalty and care for Naomi over such a long journey to a foreign land.

FOLLOWING GOD

PSALMS
GET TO KNOW THE ALL-KNOWING GOD

TEXT TRUTH

God knows everything, and we can know Him better by reading the Bible.

EXAMINE THE TEXT

PSALM 139:1-5

The book of Psalms tells us a lot about God. God shows us so much about Himself through His relationships with different people. Every verse in the book of Psalms reveals a little more about God by how He is described and how He relates to people.

When you read Psalm 139:1–5, you will see something truly wonderful about God. These verses show us how much God cares for us and how involved He is in our lives. If you look carefully through the verses again, you might notice that He knows our thoughts, our words, and our actions.

God knows those things about us because He knows everything. You might have heard Him described as omniscient. At the beginning of that word is a four-letter prefix—*omni*.

Omni means "all." There are three *omni* words you need to know: *Omniscient*, which means "all-knowing"; *omnipresent*, which means "all-present"; and *omnipotent*, which means "all-powerful." God is all-knowing, all-present, and all-powerful. When you pray, you can think the prayer in your mind because God knows your thoughts! He is amazing!

When we read psalms, we can learn about God, and we can be inspired

MEMORY VERSE

PSALM 139:1
LORD, you have searched me and known me.

PSALM WRITER

to worship Him. The psalms are praises to God. Some of them describe how people are afraid or how they need to repent. Others overflow with gratitude for the Lord. They are honest and helpful and interesting.

Here are some fun facts about the book of Psalms:

- The word *praise* appears more times in Psalms than it does in all of the rest of the books of the Bible combined!

- Psalms covers a time span of approximately one thousand years!

- If you are talking about one, it is called a psalm, but more than one are psalms.

- There are 150 psalms.

- The shortest Psalm is 117, and the longest is 119. The verse in the middle of the Bible is Psalm 118:8—right between the shortest and longest psalms!

The Bible tells us that David worshiped God through playing music and singing. David also wrote some of the poetry we find in the book of Psalms. As a shepherd, David was committed to working hard, and he used his time alone with the sheep to sing songs of praise to God.

PSALMS

The book of Psalms helps us know God better (Psalm 46:10; 100:3).

God deserves to be praised (Psalm 139:14).

- There are 594 chapters before Psalm 118:8 and 594 chapters after (594 + 594 = 1,188).

- Psalm 23 is the most well-known psalm.

- Psalm 90 is the oldest psalm. It dates back to Moses.

- The book of Psalms corresponds to the first five books of the Old Testament: Psalms 1–41 go with Genesis; Psalms 42–72 go with Exodus; Psalms 73–89 go with Leviticus; Psalms 90–106 go with Numbers; Psalms 107–150 go with Deuteronomy.

If you ever want to praise God, just open your Bible and read Psalms. You will see that He is with us in times of trouble and triumph. He loves, He forgives, He comforts, and He saves. God deserves to be praised.

PRAYER

God knows everything. He knows you very well. He knows what you need and what you want. He knows when you are sad or afraid or angry. You can talk to God about anything because He will not be surprised. Thank God for letting us know Him through the Bible. Ask God to help you know Him better and enjoy reading the Bible, especially the book of Psalms.

EXODUS
THE MIRACLE AT THE WATER

TEXT TRUTH

We can always trust God to care for our needs, even when things do not appear as we expect.

MEMORY VERSE

EXODUS 15:25

He cried out to the LORD, and the LORD showed him a tree. When he threw it into the water, the water became drinkable. The LORD made a statute and ordinance for them at Marah, and he tested them there.

EXAMINE THE TEXT

EXODUS 15:22-27

If you are familiar with the book of Exodus, you probably know about some of the exciting moments of God leading the Israelites out of slavery. You might remember baby Moses in a basket, the burning bush, the plagues, or when God gave the Ten Commandments. You probably know about God parting the Red Sea to let the Israelites escape the Egyptian soldiers. You might even know that after their escape, God fed them with bread from heaven that they called manna.

God performed another miracle before giving them manna. The Israelites had just crossed the sea after they had seen God do miraculous things over and over. They praised God.

It must have been quite a celebration, but within days they were no longer rejoicing.

Right after the excitement of having God rescue them from the Egyptians, the Israelites were grumbling. They needed water, but the river water was bitter and undrinkable. That was pretty important, but they probably could have thought of better ways to handle the problem than complaining

EXODUS

When we face unexpected problems, we should turn to God first (Exodus 15:25).

KEY POINTS

The Lord is generous and cares for our needs (Exodus 15:25).

God wants His people to listen and obey (Exodus 15:26).

to Moses. Although the complaints were to Moses, they were actually about God. The way they responded to not having water was part of a long pattern of complaining and wavering.

Moses turned to God for help. That should have been the obvious way for the Israelites to deal with any unusual circumstance. When Moses cried out to God, he was given a branch to toss into the water. The water was now good for the Israelites to drink! It might not have been as exciting as racing away from chariots, but every miracle from God is pretty fascinating.

God then told the Israelites that if they listened and obeyed, they would not face disease because He is the healer. What a blessing! God did not have to make that offer to the Israelites; He deserves to be obeyed no matter what. He was not making a deal with them or trying to motivate them. He was giving them a gift.

This promise He made to the Israelites was a special promise to them throughout their journey. It does not apply the same way today.

Disobeying God will not cause you to get sick, and obeying Him will not cause you to get well. Disease and illness exist because sin damaged the entire world. We cannot always control healing, but we can always trust that the Healer is in control.

When you read Exodus 15:27, you can see that God led the Israelites to a place with plenty of water and comfort. It was probably luxurious. They might not have complained if they had remembered His previous miracles and generosity!

We can learn from this example. We can be grateful for the things God provides. We can trust that He is in control. When you think of all that you are learning about God, you might want to remember that today's verses show us that He is patient, He provides, He is powerful, He is generous, He has authority, and He cares.

PRAYER

Moses trusted God to guide the Israelites. When they encountered a problem, Moses turned to God. We can trust God and turn to Him when we have needs and problems too. Feel free to thank the Lord for caring about your needs. You can tell Him about any needs you have right now. Ask Him to help you trust Him in whatever circumstances you face.

JEBEL MUSA

Jebel Musa (Mount of Moses) is the most popular location known as Mount Sinai. Moses and the people were at Mount Sinai when God gave them the Law.

LEVITICUS

UNHOLY PEOPLE NEED A HOLY SACRIFICE

TEXT TRUTH

There is a high price to pay for sin, and Jesus paid the price.

EXAMINE THE TEXT

LEVITICUS 16

The book of Leviticus is full of ceremonies and regulations that do not apply to our world today. They might not always seem interesting or important, but they definitely are. In fact, some of the most important things we can know, such as atonement, are emphasized in the book of Leviticus. You might have heard the word *atonement* before. It actually means that guilt is removed and the eternal impact of sin is repaired.

If you spend a few minutes looking through Leviticus 16, you will see that this chapter describes the Day of Atonement, a yearly ritual to atone for individual and national sins. The Lord gave very specific instructions for Aaron. There were goats, linen garments, a bull, coals, and all sorts of detailed plans for every step of the process. It was a rigorous ritual that revealed the unholiness of the people and illustrated the need for a perfect and permanent sacrifice. Can you guess what sacrifice would replace this annual ceremony? If your answer is Jesus' sacrifice on the cross, you are right! He was the perfect and permanent sacrifice that atoned for sin.

MEMORY VERSE

LEVITICUS 16:30

Atonement will be made for you on this day to cleanse you, and you will be clean from all your sins before the LORD.

HIGH PRIEST

In Old Testament times, the high priest served in the tabernacle. He would offer sacrifices for the people's sins. Jesus is our great high priest who gives us access to God's grace and mercy.

God's standard is perfection. The rituals described in the book of Leviticus are helpful to show that people are imperfect. No one could make it through a year without needing atonement for sin. In fact, God had given the people requirements for other daily sacrifices to atone for their sin.

You might be wondering why sacrifices had to be made. It seems sad that animals died during those ceremonies. Death is the high price of sin. Sin is terrible and requires judgment. Sometimes we think our sins are no big deal, but God never sees sin that way. He will not allow sin to go unpunished. Every year the animals were offered to pay for sin, but they were not enough. The sacrifices had to be repeated over and over. When Jesus died on the cross, He paid for sin forever. His sacrifice was enough!

LEVITICUS

God is perfect and requires perfect obedience (Leviticus 22:20, 31).

People do not meet God's standard and need atonement for sin (Leviticus 16:30).

Jesus atoned for sin perfectly and permanently (1 Peter 3:18).

Maybe you did not realize before you started reading that a book in the Old Testament would point to Jesus, but that is what happens in the entire Bible. God loves us enough to show us who He is throughout every book of the Bible. Chapter 16 in the book of Leviticus shows us that we need atonement for our sin, and Jesus is the answer. Because He was the perfect sacrifice, we can be forgiven.

PRAYER

We are no different from the people who lived during the time of Leviticus. We are all sinners who need atonement. We depend on God for forgiveness. Thank the Lord for showing us our need for Him and making a way for us to be forgiven. If you have sin in your life, you can ask for forgiveness and ask God to help you turn to Him instead of sin in the future.

1 CORINTHIANS
IN REMEMBRANCE OF JESUS

TEXT TRUTH

The Lord's Supper is meaningful to Christians because it commemorates Jesus' sacrifice.

MEMORY VERSE

1 CORINTHIANS 11:28
Let a person examine himself; in this way let him eat the bread and drink from the cup.

EXAMINE THE TEXT

1 CORINTHIANS 11:23-29

In these verses Paul describes the focus and importance of the Lord's Supper. Unfortunately, the church at Corinth was not gathering in remembrance of Jesus. Instead, they were indulging in gluttony and disgracing the Lord's Supper. Paul's guidance for them has helped many churches throughout many generations to remember why the Lord's Supper is so meaningful.

Paul mentions the night Jesus was betrayed just before He died. Jesus shared a meal with His disciples and told them to eat and drink in remembrance. That is why we still share the Lord's Supper. We remember Christ's sacrifice on the cross. His body is represented by the bread, and His blood is represented by the drink.

There is no specific guidance on how the Lord's Supper should be served, so different churches participate in different ways. Some serve it every week, while others do it only once a year. Some invite only the members of their church to participate, but others have no restrictions. Some pass the elements around on plates; others have people go to tables to retrieve them. Some churches call it the Lord's Supper while others call it Communion.

1 CORINTHIANS

The Lord's Supper is a remembrance of Jesus' sacrifice on the cross (1 Corinthians 11:24-25).

Christians identify their unity with Christ when they participate in the Lord's Supper (1 Corinthians 11:26).

As long as the focus is on remembering Jesus' sacrifice and reflecting on what it means for us, the differences do not matter.

If you ever wonder whether you should participate in the Lord's Supper, here are some things to help you:

1. Get permission. You should not do anything without first asking for your parents' approval. They might have restrictions you are not aware of. There are also some churches that discourage anyone from participating if they have not been baptized, reached a certain age, become an official member of the church, or other similar reasons.

2. Understand what it means. To understand the reason for the Lord's Supper, you have to understand the purpose for what happened with Jesus on the cross.

3. Evaluate your motives. Consider why you want to participate.

Are you only interested because you feel like you are missing out on something? The Lord's Supper is a special reflection on the sacrifice of Jesus. He is the only worthy motive for participation.

4. Examine yourself. The Lord's Supper is a unique opportunity for Christians to identify their unity with Christ. Going to church does not make a person a Christian. People are saved by God's grace through faith in Jesus. Are you saved and forgiven of your sin? If you are not sure, you are probably not ready to take the Lord's Supper.

The Lord's Supper is a very special experience that should be taken seriously. Even if you have taken it in the past, you will want to think of what it means and whether you are truly ready to participate. When it is time for you to take the Lord's Supper, you can use the opportunity to remember what Jesus' sacrifice means for you.

LORD'S SUPPER

At the Last Supper, Jesus drank from a cup and broke bread with the apostles. The Bible tells us that we should follow His example to remember Jesus and His sacrifice. The bread represents His body and the cup represents the blood He shed on the cross.

PRAYER

It is not always obvious when we should participate in certain activities. The Lord's Supper is one of those unusual events that has special meaning and requires special consideration. You can ask God to help you examine your relationship with Him to know when you are ready to participate in the Lord's Supper. Thank God for sending Jesus to die on the cross, and ask Him to help you understand why the Lord's Supper matters to Christians.

2 CORINTHIANS

TEST YOURSELF

TEXT TRUTH

It is important to examine your life to be sure you truly trust, love, and follow Jesus.

EXAMINE THE TEXT

2 CORINTHIANS 13:5-6

Let's imagine that you are sitting in church listening to your pastor's preaching.

MEMORY VERSE

2 CORINTHIANS 13:5
Test yourselves to see if you are in the faith. Examine yourselves. Or do you yourselves not recognize that Jesus Christ is in you?—unless you fail the test.

You hear the message of Jesus and how His death on the cross provided the payment for sin. You repent and trust Jesus as your Savior, receiving His gift of salvation. Later in your life you run into some struggles and hard times. How you handle those hard times shows your commitment to following God.

Following Jesus is more than a single prayer or a few years of obedience. Those who truly love and trust Him will reflect it throughout their entire lives. Paul sent letters to guide, correct, assist, and sometimes challenge the people in the church at Corinth. He cared for them and wanted to help them live for God. In 2 Corinthians 13:5–6, Paul encourages people to examine themselves and warns about failing the test. This warning was sent out of concern because he knew the people were not always obedient to God's Word.

It would be easy to read these verses and think they only apply to people who openly reject God or have never been to church before, but these verses are important for all of us to read and apply. Remember, Paul is writing to church members! If you examine your life and discover that you are truly following God, you might see areas where you can avoid sin or grow in holiness. That is a great result of testing your faith.

If you examine your life and discover that you are not truly following God, you might see that you need to repent and have faith. You might realize that you understand salvation better as you get older, and you want to be clear about your relationship with God. Those are great results of testing your faith too!

The Banias Waterfall near Caesarea Philippi is the largest waterfall in Israel. Jesus and His disciples were in Caesarea Philippi near this waterfall in Banias when He gave the disciples a test—He asked His disciples to tell Him who He is. Who did the disciples say Jesus is?

THE TEST

2 CORINTHIANS

KEY POINTS

Examine your life to determine if you truly love and trust God (2 Corinthians 13:5).

Get to know God through the Bible, and you will know what He wants for you and from you (Romans 15:4).

Every verse in Scripture helps us, even if they do not seem to apply. These verses are for you as much as they were for the people in Corinth.

The most important thing you can do to test yourself is to read the Bible. If you learn what is in the Bible, you will learn who God is, what He wants for you, and what He wants from you. When you know God, you can understand His grace and how it impacts your life.

PRAYER

We can be grateful for the Bible because it helps us understand God. It can also help you understand your relationship with God. When you thank the Lord for the Bible, ask Him to show you things in it that you need to know. Ask Him to help you use the Bible to examine your faith, and ask Him to help you love Him, trust Him, and live for Him.

2 SAMUEL

A CHOSEN KING

TEXT TRUTH

David became king as part of God's sovereign plan.

EXAMINE THE TEXT

2 SAMUEL 5:1-3; 7:8, 16, 28

Second Samuel 5:1–3 shows us a very special moment in history. All the tribes of Israel were represented, and they were united in welcoming David as king. In the first verse, they made sure David understood they would protect and support him as if they were part of his family or, more literally, part of his body. In the second verse, they recognized his military leadership, and they acknowledged God's decision to make him king. When you read the book of 1 Samuel, you will see that God sent Samuel to find David when David was only a boy. He was watching sheep while his brothers were being considered to be the next king. When Samuel looked at all the brothers, he knew none of them had been chosen by God. Once David was brought in from the field, Samuel announced God's selection and anointed him in front of his brothers.

David's appointed rise from shepherd to king is referenced in different places in the Bible. Not only does this part of David's story show God's sovereignty, but it also connects to a different kind of king and shepherd. Read 2 Samuel 7:8 and 16 and see if David's story makes you think of anyone else.

MEMORY VERSE

2 SAMUEL 7:28
Lord GOD, you are God; your words are true, and you have promised this good thing to your servant.

2 SAMUEL

David's life pointed to Jesus (2 Samuel 7:16).

KEY POINTS

God had a plan for David's life (2 Samuel 7:28).

God has a plan for your life (Jeremiah 29:11).

Did it make you think of Jesus? There are many things in David's life that show a picture of what was and is to come with Jesus. Even though many of the connections might not have been obvious at the time, we can clearly see God's design as we look back through the Bible.

Have you ever watched a movie that you had already seen before? The second time we see something we know what to expect. We know what to watch for. We can pay closer attention to the details. David was one of many people God used to prepare everyone for Jesus. He wanted the world to know what to watch for.

It was no accident that David became king. God had a plan for his life all along. What is God's plan for your life? Are you able to see what He is doing now, or will you have to look back later to notice? Is He preparing you for something? Is He using you to prepare others for something? It might not be easy to understand what God is doing in your life, but you can be confident that He has a plan. Maybe

you will never be a king, but your life matters to God just as much as David's.

Second Samuel 7:28 should cause you to think of who God is. The Lord is in charge of everything. He can do whatever He wants, and He has chosen to do something in your life. If you have not trusted God for your salvation, you can assume that is His first priority for your life. Have faith in God's grace to forgive, because Jesus died on the cross to pay for your sin.

FRIEND TO DAVID

PRAYER

God's plan included making David a king. His plan includes you in some way too. You can trust God and thank Him for including you in His sovereign plan. He can help you see what He wants for your life and help you trust His plan. Ask Him for guidance or courage or anything else you need to be able to follow Him.

Nathan was a prophet in the royal court. He served both King David and King Solomon. In the Old Testament, prophets were people used by God to share special, true messages with His people. Nathan helped David to see God's plan for him.

67

1 CHRONICLES
GIVE GENEROUSLY TO GOD

TEXT TRUTH

We should give generously as part of our worship and honor of God.

MEMORY VERSE

1 CHRONICLES 29:13
Now therefore, our God, we give you thanks and praise your glorious name.

EXAMINE THE TEXT

1 CHRONICLES 29:1-5, 11-13

There are several parts of King David's life mentioned throughout the book of 1 Chronicles, but one story in particular shows him honoring God with humility and generosity. David wanted to build a temple for God. He began preparations and made a plan. However, God had a different plan. Because David was a warrior who had shed much blood, he was not permitted to lead the building project. Instead, his son Solomon was chosen to oversee the building of the temple.

David recognized that the temple was for God and would be erected the way God wanted. David empha-sized God's will when he publicly announced the plan in 1 Chronicles 29:1. David also mentioned Solomon's youth and inexperience. Why do you think he did that? Do you suppose it was to show that God did not need human strength and ability or that they would all need to help Solomon? If you remember, David was chosen as king when he was only a boy. So he knew that youth and inexperience would not keep God from using people. However, in this case, it was also important for the people to take part.

In 1 Chronicles 29:2–5, David encouraged giving by being an example to the people. He gave abun-dantly! As a king, he had access to the riches collected from battle. Not only did David give generously from those riches, but he also gave from his own personal wealth. He wanted to show his devotion to God and his commitment to building the temple, and to be an example for others to follow. Others followed David's example. They gave generously and joyfully. It was more than a building project. It was an opportunity to honor and worship God.

After the offerings for the temple were received, everyone gathered to rejoice and praise God. When you read 1 Chronicles 29:11–13, you will see what David said to the Lord. David recognized that giving generously to the Lord was a privilege. All things belong to God, and He deserves all

OBEY BY GIVING

Coins such as these shekels, the most common coin used by the Jews, were often given for the temple tax.

1 CHRONICLES

KEY POINTS

David knew the temple was for God, so he gave generously (1 Chronicles 29:1).

David's contribution inspired others to give (1 Chronicles 29:6).

Everyone rejoiced in giving to the Lord (1 Chronicles 29:9).

things.

The opportunity to contribute to the Lord's work is a blessing from the Lord.

How are you able to give to God? If you do not have money and are looking for ways to give generously to the Lord, there are many ways to contribute to what God is doing. David's gift included things like metals, stones, and wood. You probably do not have those things lying around your room, but we all have things we can give generously. Something as simple as a smile can be used by God. If you go to a small group on Sunday mornings, you can stand by the door as your friends enter and greet them with a welcoming smile. Your God-honoring example can inspire others to joyfully participate in the service. Of course, we should always be willing to give money and items when there is a need that honors God, but you can honor God with any offering you have, even a smile.

PRAYER

David recognized that it was important to give from his own wealth in contribution to the temple. He was an example of generosity and prioritized the mission God had called him to. You will have opportunities to support things that God is doing. Ask Him to help you decide whether to give money, time, prayers, or some other contribution. You can ask God if you need help knowing when to give generously as an act of worship and as an example to others.

GALATIANS
GUILTY BUT JUSTIFIED

TEXT TRUTH

Even though we are all guilty of sin, we can be justified by faith in Christ.

EXAMINE THE TEXT

GALATIANS 2:11-18

When a judge decides guilt or innocence in a legal trial, the judge uses evidence to make a decision. That is not the way God makes His judgments. All are sinners. The Lord does not need to weigh the evidence. He knows that we are guilty. If everyone is guilty of sin, why would God ever declare anyone not guilty? You will find the answer in Galatians 2:16. The word *justified* is repeated a few times in that verse. It is a legal term that means someone has been declared not guilty. So that verse tells us that sinners are declared not guilty by faith in Christ.

That is exciting news! If we were judged based on the legal evidence, we would all be guilty. Instead, we are justified based on faith in Christ.

Paul had to explain that to the people in Galatia. Some people called Judaizers insisted that Gentiles had to follow Jewish law before they could follow Jesus. Galatians 2:11–14 shows the kinds of problems that were being caused by this false teaching.

Cephas, better known as Peter, was a Jew who followed Christ. Eating with the Gentiles suggested that he accepted them as fellow believers.

MEMORY VERSE

GALATIANS 2:18

If I rebuild those things that I tore down, I show myself to be a lawbreaker.

GALATIANS

Because of Jesus, we are not judged by the law but by faith (Galatians 2:16).

Jesus' sacrifice was enough to justify sinners (Galatians 3:24).

Sinners are justified by faith in Jesus (Galatians 2:16).

When the Judaizers came around, he was intimidated and refused to eat with the Gentiles. Paul confronted Peter and used it as an example to discourage hypocrisy. He wanted everyone to know what the group taught was false and divisive.

The Jews had been given the law many, many years earlier. It was a very important part of life. Some of them did not understand that when Jesus died on the cross, He fulfilled the law. That is why we are not judged by how well we obey the law but by our faith in Christ. Remember, we all disobey the law. We all sin. If we were judged by the law, we would all be in really big trouble.

In Galatians 2:18 Paul was telling the Christians that if they returned to the law, they were acting as if Jesus had not died on the cross and fulfilled the law. It means the same thing for us today. Jesus accomplished every-thing that was necessary to forgive sin. If we add extra requirements to His sacrifice, we are acting as though He was not enough. Jesus' sacrifice was enough to save you from the punishment of sin. You can have faith in Christ.

Antonia Fortress is the likely location where Jesus was held before He was crucified, and Paul was taken there too. The fortress had passageways that connected it with temple courts. It had 3 towers 86 feet high, and one 120 feet high. It was the place King Herod lived and Roman troops stayed.

PRAYER

Because we are all sinners, we are all guilty before God. Now that you know there is hope in Jesus, you can talk to God about your faith. The Judaizers did not understand what Jesus had accomplished on behalf of sinners. You can ask God to help you avoid their mistakes. You can ask Him to help you understand that Jesus' sacrifice was enough to justify sinners and to help you put your faith in Christ.

JAMES
LIVE YOUR FAITH

TEXT TRUTH

Genuine faith in God will include obedience to God's Word.

EXAMINE THE TEXT

JAMES 2:14-19

Do you have a friend who will let you know when you have something stuck between your teeth? Everyone needs a friend like that. It is good to have a person who will help you out when you do not realize there is a problem. Of course, it can be embarrassing to have someone notice something about us that we need to correct. Sometimes we do not want others to see our flaws or we want to ignore them ourselves. That happens with the book of James. Some people do not like to read it because it can be uncomfortable. This book will make you think of how you live and what that proves about what you believe.

You might remember from the book of Galatians how people taught that certain actions and behaviors were necessary to become a Christian or to remain a Christian. Paul corrected that wrong teaching and explained that there are no behaviors that can save; only faith in Christ saves. Today, as you read from the book of James, you will see that behaviors are the topic again. Both books agree that salvation is God's gift through faith in Jesus, but James insists that when you have faith you will live differently.

MEMORY VERSE

JAMES 2:17

In the same way faith, if it doesn't have works, is dead by itself.

Many early Christians were immersed in the Jordan River to show that they repented of their sins and trusted in Jesus. Baptism is a symbol of a new life as a Christian, but we are also commanded to live our lives according to God's Word to show our faith.

In James 2:14–16, James points out that knowing someone has needs but not being willing to help makes the concern for that person meaningless; it has no impact on the person's need. In verse 17, James says if faith does not impact life, it is meaningless. In other words, it is not real faith. You can say all the right things, but without action it is dead.

James 2:18 explains that genuine faith changes the way we live. It will not simply be something we think. It will be visible in our lives.

Now for the really uncomfortable verse, James 2:19. This verse is a warning. James explains that knowing things about God is not evidence of salvation. Even the demons know things about God! Evidence of salvation comes through a person's actions.

It is pretty clear from these verses that faith will be evident in the way we live. As uncomfortable as it is, we have to consider that truth when we look at our own lives. What does your life reveal about your faith?

JAMES

Those who have true faith in God will express it by how they live (James 2:17-18).

KEY POINTS

Living for God requires action. No verse or chapter or book is all by itself in the Bible. It all fits together to help us understand everything God wants us to know. So when we put the teaching about faith together, we learn something very important. Our behavior will not save us, but it will reveal whether we are saved.

Genuine faith will result in actions (James 2:17-18).

PRAYER

One of the reasons God gave us the Bible is so that we will understand how to live for Him. When you think of everything you have learned about faith, ask yourself if you have been living a genuine faith or a dead faith. You can talk to God about having a living faith in your life. Ask God to give you a true faith and to help you live the way He wants you to live.

MARK

JESUS CARES. TRUST JESUS.

TEXT TRUTH

Jesus taught many things in many ways, including how to care for people and have true faith.

EXAMINE THE TEXT

MARK 3:1-6; 10:13-16

The Bible is very interesting, and many people would probably agree that the book of Mark is one of the most exciting books to read. There are so many different events described in Mark that it feels like one adventure after another. Maybe it is fascinating because every chapter illustrates Jesus' time on earth. We can see all the ways to learn from His example and how His days were filled with teaching, serving, and loving others.

Some Bibles include descriptions before chapters or passages that tell what the particular sections are about. If you turn the pages of your Bible and look for those titles or descriptions throughout the book of Mark, you will probably notice all the different events this book describes. Were you familiar with some of them?

This book is filled with things to learn about Jesus' time on earth. One particular story is in Mark 3:1–6. There are several things we can learn from that encounter, but here are three specific things. First, the religious leaders wanted to destroy Jesus.

MEMORY VERSE

MARK 10:15
Truly I tell you, whoever does not receive the kingdom of God like a little child will never enter it.

MARK

We can learn many things from Jesus' time on earth (Mark 10:45).

KEY POINTS

Jesus cares for people (Mark 3:5).

Jesus wants us to completely trust Him with our lives (Mark 10:15).

This was one of a handful of encounters where they tried to catch Jesus doing something wrong or trick Him into contradicting Himself. They never could, so they were angry and tried to figure out another way to destroy Him. Second, Jesus healed the man's withered hand. That was a miracle! We can read every day about the miracles of Jesus, but they will never stop being amazing. Third, Jesus cares. He cares about truth, obedience, and people. The religious leaders were wrong, and their plans did not follow God's commands. They did not concern themselves with the man's struggles or needs.

Mark 10:13–16 is another example of how Jesus showed what is most important to God. This time it was not a group of religious leaders trying to destroy Him. Instead, it was His own disciples who misunderstood His priorities. They were keeping the children from approaching Jesus. When He insisted that they should let the children come to Him, it was an

expression of kindness, but it was also more than that. Jesus used it as an example of faith.

These were probably babies or very young children who were being brought to Jesus. Because babies are completely dependent on their parents, they must trust them in every way. That is the type of trust Jesus wants from us. That is a pure faith. We can learn a lot from Jesus' many encounters with people while He was on the earth. Hopefully you will enjoy reading the book of Mark and seeing the many ways Jesus wants us to love others and trust Him.

PRAYER

The many stories of Jesus' encounters with people while He was on earth teach us so much about Him. His love for people is obvious in every chapter of Mark. We can be thankful to the Lord for giving us the Bible so we can know Jesus and learn from His time on earth. Pray and ask God to help you love others the way He does and have the faith Jesus described.

HEALING POWER

The symbol for first aid actually comes from the ancient Romans. The snake and staff are from the ancient god Asclepius. He was the Roman god of healing, and people would sleep in temples dedicated to him and pray for him to heal them. But we know he was a false god. Only Jesus has true healing power!

1 TIMOTHY

PRAY FOR ALL

TEXT TRUTH

We can participate in an important part of worship and service to the church when we pray.

EXAMINE THE TEXT

1 TIMOTHY 2:1-3

The book of 1 Timothy mainly describes ways to organize and manage the church. It helps guide decisions because it shows what is important to consider in the leadership and function of a church. That probably seems like it might not have a lot to do with a regular church member, especially a kid, but it is important for everyone to know how a biblical church should function. Not only does it help us understand how to support, encourage, and hold one another accountable, but it also teaches us important things about God and how we can serve Him within the church. One particular way is to pray.

When you read 1 Timothy 2:1–3, you will see the different ways prayer is described. Those are not necessarily different prayers that should be made. Instead, they are different attitudes and approaches to prayer. Here are some things to think about when we pray:

- We align ourselves with God in faith.
- We honor God by trusting His will and His plan.
- When we ask for something it can be in appreciation for His generosity.

MEMORY VERSE

1 TIMOTHY 2:1
First of all, then, I urge that petitions, prayers, intercessions, and thanksgivings be made for everyone.

PLACE OF PRAYER

- We can pray as an act of worship.

- We can persistently turn to God with ongoing needs or desires.

Those examples teach us that prayer is not a list of statements or requests. We are able to talk to God in a variety of ways that show our dependence on Him and our respect for Him.

In 1 Timothy 2:1–3, Paul wrote to Timothy that prayer is pleasing and good. Paul encouraged praying for leaders. That is always a good idea because they are not only in great need of prayer, but they also have a lot of influence. He urged prayer for all people. Every person has different needs and desires. Your prayers for them could impact their lives in unseen ways.

The Beautiful Gate was the entrance to the temple complex in Jerusalem. Many people walked through this gate on their way to pray and worship God. Some people believe this is the location of the Beautiful Gate. In Bible times the gate was made of solid bronze and would dazzle and shine brightly in the sun. No wonder they called it beautiful!

1 TIMOTHY

Prayer is a way to worship and serve God (1 Timothy 2:3).

The church needs prayer in order to function properly (1 Timothy 2:2).

Did you ever think that maybe your role in the church might include praying for others? You are not ready to be a leader in the church. You are not able to make decisions about ministry, but you are very important in the church. Be creative to find different ways to contribute to the church as a kid. Prayer is a great place to start.

You can contribute to the church by praying for the members of your church and the leadership of your church (1 Timothy 2:2).

PRAYER

Prayer is an important part of the Christian life. When we pray, we are communicating with God as an act of worship. When you think of how God wants you to pray for others, you might want to make a list or a plan to stay organized. When you thank God for the opportunity to talk to Him and the opportunity to pray for others, you can ask Him to help you know how to pray and show you people you can pray for.

2 TIMOTHY

SCRIPTURE IS FROM GOD

TEXT TRUTH

The Bible is the inspired Word of God, and we can trust it as the source of truth.

EXAMINE THE TEXT

2 TIMOTHY 3:16-17

Imagine that you go to church with someone every week, and he always seems to know the Bible stories and the verses very well. He impresses everyone with his behavior because he is always friendly and respectful. He appears to live according to the Bible. Would it be wrong if he also follows another book that he considers just as holy as the Bible? It would. The Bible is the only truly holy book. It is the only thing that has been directly inspired by God. It is His message to us. No other writings will ever be as important or true as the Bible.

When you read 2 Timothy 3:16–17, you will see that verse 16 says all Scripture is breathed out by God; it is saying that God directly gave the

MEMORY VERSE

2 TIMOTHY 3:16
All Scripture is inspired by God.

message of the Bible. He gave the entire Bible message as the perfect source of truth. What this means for us is that we can trust the Bible. We do not need other books to show us more, because this is the complete message from God. Any other books must support what is in the Bible or they are not true.

Nothing is equal to the Bible. Even very helpful books that agree with what is in the Bible are not as important or as special. The Bible is holy.

2 TIMOTHY

The Bible is God's direct message to us (2 Timothy 3:16–17).

KEY POINTS

The Bible is complete and holy and true (2 Timothy 3:16–17).

We need the Bible to know God and know how to live (2 Timothy 3:16–17).

If you look again at 2 Timothy 3:16–17, you will notice that the Bible equips us for everything we need in life. The Bible shows us God's standard. It shows us what we need to know about Him. It shows us how to live and that we are sinners who require forgiveness. The Bible is our resource that guides us in every way.

Do you ever wonder why the Bible includes so many stories of people sinning? Because we are all sinners! God is able to show us how to live through the examples of others. He is also able to show us repentance and forgiveness and faith through those same examples. God did not remove the sinful parts of the stories in the Bible because He uses them to teach us who He is and how much we need Him.

What is your favorite part of the Bible? Although the entire Bible is important to each of us, it is not unusual to have a favorite book or story. God wants us to enjoy the Bible. Sin can cause us not to enjoy the Bible, but God is always willing to help us overcome anything that keeps us from turning to His Word.

Do you ever talk to your friends about the Bible? It is common for people to talk about interesting stories. Bible stories are the most adventurous and exciting stories of all. Not only are they entertaining, they also have great purpose. The things you learn from the Bible can be shared and enjoyed and trusted. We can all rely on Scripture to guide us through life.

PRAYER

We should all ask ourselves how often we turn to the Bible to know God better or to know how He wants us to live. If you do not depend on the Bible, you can talk to God about it and ask for His help. God wants us to love His Word. Thank the Lord for giving us the Bible, and ask Him for better understanding, proper conviction, and enjoyment as you read it.

THE BIBLE

The most famous Bible in the world is the Gutenberg Bible. It was made in 1455, in Mainz, Germany by Johann Gutenberg, who invented the printing press.

TITUS
ETERNAL LIFE AND THE SAVIOR

TEXT TRUTH

God is kind to offer salvation and eternal life.

EXAMINE THE TEXT

TITUS 3:4-7

The book of Titus is so short that it can be tempting to read the entire thing quickly. This book has plenty of helpful guidance and truth even though it is only three chapters. When you read Titus 3:4–7, you will see that plenty of important things can be packed into a few verses.

If you look through each verse carefully, you will see the things it tells us about God and what He has done for us. One of the most important things is that God is good and kind. He offers us everything because of His kindness. If you want to look a little closer at the verses, here are a few questions you can ask yourself as you read them:

- What is God called (verse 4)?
- What did God do (verse 5)? Why?

MEMORY VERSE

TITUS 3:7

Having been justified by his grace, we may become heirs with the hope of eternal life.

- Who is poured out on us (verses 5 and 6)?
- How are we justified (verse 7)?

Taking time to notice all the information offered in a Bible verse can show you so much more than you might have noticed if you rushed through it. You can look for those types of things every time you read the Bible. It will help you see everything God wants to show you in the Bible.

BEGINNING AND END

Alpha and Omega are the first and last letters of the Greek alphabet. God says that He is the alpha and the omega—He is forever. This picture of a box from the AD 500s has an alpha and omega on either side of it.

Hopefully, as you were reading and studying these verses, you noticed all the important things about God and salvation. There is so much packed into those verses! When Paul wrote this book to Titus, he wanted to emphasize God's saving grace. Since we cannot behave well enough to earn forgiveness, it is only God who can save. He is kind and merciful to forgive sin by grace through faith in Jesus.

Jesus was only on earth for a while, then He returned to heaven. God did not want us to be alone, so He gave us the Holy Spirit. Because of the Holy Spirit, we now have God with us here on earth in a different way. The Holy Spirit can be a comfort. He can help us understand and apply what we read in the Bible. He can also give us courage and help us tell others the message of Jesus.

TITUS

God is the Savior (Titus 3:4-6).

God offers salvation by His grace through faith in Jesus (Titus 3:5-6).

God is so generous! It is very loving for God to offer such gifts through salvation. Another gift is mentioned in verse 7: eternal life. The Holy Spirit is given to us when we are saved, which means God is with us. He will never leave us. After our time on earth is through, we will be face-to-face with God in heaven. That is what it means to have eternal life, to be with God forever. Praise the Lord for His saving grace and eternal life!

Because of God's kindness, we can have eternal life (Titus 3:5).

PRAYER

There are many important things to remember from today's verses, but one of the most important things is that God is willing to save sinners. Not only does His sacrifice on the cross allow us to be with God, it allows us to be with Him forever! When you thank God for His kindness and His grace, for being forgiving and for offering us salvation through Jesus, ask Him to give you a true saving faith and eternal life.

AMOS
THE LORD IS HIS NAME

TEXT TRUTH

We should never allow sin to distract us from who God is.

MEMORY VERSE

AMOS 9:6

He builds his upper chambers in the heavens and lays the foundation of his vault on the earth. He summons the water of the sea and pours it out over the surface of the earth. The LORD is his name.

EXAMINE THE TEXT

AMOS 9:5-6

Sometimes we enjoy thinking of God's kindness and patience so much that we forget how He views sin. Sin angers God. He does not ignore sin, but He is patient to allow us the opportunity to repent. People take advantage of His patience. That is what happened with the Israelites. You might remember that the people of Israel had a pattern. They would serve God, sin, face the consequences of sin, repent, then God would deliver them. The book of Amos illustrates a season of time when Israel had been sinning against God and He warned them that consequences were on the way.

The people of Israel were not looking forward to the consequences of their sin. They even asked Amos to leave and go prophesy somewhere else. They did not want to hear the news of God's judgment. As much as we might want to criticize the Israelites, we can all relate to their pattern. They were sinners who kept returning to sin. We are all sinners

AMOS

KEY POINTS

The Israelites did not remain committed to God (Amos 4:8).

Amos warned Israel that they would be punished for their sin (Amos 3:1–2).

We should not forget that the Lord is the one true God (Amos 9:6).

who return to sin. It is only with God's help that we turn away from sin.

Unfortunately for the Israelite people, in this circumstance God used punishment to turn them back to Him. It was a harsh consequence of their sin, but it was loving. Even though we might not usually think of punishment as loving, God's punishment is always loving. He corrects those He loves, and He uses consequences to guide and purify His people.

God had plans for Israel, so He did not leave them in their sin. Even though the Israelites had not been faithful to serve and worship the one and only true God, He was still in control. He was still God. Amos 9:5–6 expresses God's authority and ends with a powerful statement of God's identity.

The people of Israel had been caught up in the appearance of worshiping God while they had actually turned away from Him. They followed many of the rituals and traditions of the law, but they did not follow God. Instead, they indulged in idolatry.

The law had been given as a tool to show the people of Israel their great need for God. Their obedience to the law was not a way to get God to love them more. It was a way to live out their commitment to God. Somehow they began to believe that as long as they remained within the limits of the law, they were obeying God. Their sin had distracted them from truly worshiping God.

They no longer noticed the one and only true God. Maybe that is why verse 6 ends with an introduction. God is reminding everyone who He is. The warnings in the book of Amos reveal quite a bit about God. He is the leader who controls nations. He is patient. He punishes sin. He is faithful. He is righteous. He is Lord.

GOD'S POWER

Amos wrote about the powerful God who created the earth and has complete control over it. God laid the foundations of the earth and poured the waters of the seas over it.

PRAYER

We can learn from the Israelites' example not to ever lose sight of God. If you do things that appear to serve God but are not really for the right reasons, you can ask God to help you truly worship Him in everything you do. God is patient and merciful. If you ask, He can help you turn from sin, appreciate His patience, and never take His grace and forgiveness for granted.

HOSEA
SIN, CONSEQUENCES, FORGIVENESS

TEXT TRUTH

God repeatedly forgave the Israelites because even though they were not faithful, He is faithful.

MEMORY VERSE

HOSEA 13:4

I have been the LORD your God ever since the land of Egypt; you know no God but me, and no Savior exists besides me.

EXAMINE THE TEXT

HOSEA 12:5-6; 13:4

In case you have ever wondered what the words *Minor Prophets* mean, they are twelve books in the Bible that describe Israel's unfaithfulness to God while at the same time offer a glimpse into what is to come through Jesus. The Minor Prophets are Hosea, Joel, Amos, Obadiah, Jonah, Micah, Nahum, Habakkuk, Zephaniah, Haggai, Zechariah, and Malachi. They are called Minor Prophets because their books are shorter than the books called the Major Prophets, which are Isaiah, Jeremiah, Lamentations, Ezekiel, and Daniel. The books of the Minor Prophets do not contain as much information or teaching as many other books in the Bible, but they are just as important, and they reveal important truths about God.

The book of Hosea compares an unhappy marriage with the unfaithfulness of the Israelites. In the story, a wife is not committed to her husband and does not honor her promise to him. He forgives her, but she keeps turning away from him. That is exactly what happened with the Israelites.

You probably realize by now that Israel had a problem with rebellion. They kept repeating the pattern of sin and relying on God's forgiveness. Unfortunately, the consequences of their sin put them in difficult circumstances over and over again. They depended on God to rescue them from their enemies and forgive them of their sin. He was kind and faithful to deliver them.

How do you think God felt when the Israelites sinned against Him? God was saddened and disappointed over the betrayal of His people, not only because He deserved their loyalty, but also because He knew that the Israelites were causing terrible consequences for themselves.

Why do you think God continued to rescue the people of Israel? There was nothing special that made the Israelites worthy of God's forgiveness. He took care of them because He had made a promise to them.

Do you see the Latin inscription on the water fountain below? The words are from Psalm 51. The psalmist cried out to God, asking to be purified and forgiven of his sin. God promises us in the Bible that if we repent of our sins and trust in Jesus, He will forgive us. God always keeps His promises!

GOD FORGIVES!

93

HOSEA

He would not abandon them. In other words, God repeatedly rescued the people of Israel because He is faithful and good.

In Hosea 12:5–6, God is identified as the sovereign leader. The people are encouraged to return to God and stay faithful to Him. That is a message for all of us. Verse 6 basically tells us to depend on God, live for Him, and trust Him. Do you? God deserves our love and loyalty. Hosea 13:4 tells us that there is no other God. He is the Savior. What a privilege it is to know the one true God!

The Israelites were not faithful to God, but He is always faithful (Hosea 11:7-9).

KEY POINTS

God deserves our faithfulness (Hosea 12:5-6).

PRAYER

There is a lot we can learn from the example of Israel's betrayal. It shows us how to avoid the same pattern of sin and reveals God's faithfulness and mercy to forgive. Thank God for the examples we have in the Bible to help us live for Him. Thank the Lord for teaching us of His love and ask for help to remain faithful to Him and avoid sin.

JONAH

THE GOD OF SECOND CHANCES

TEXT TRUTH

When we repent of our disobedience, God is merciful and gives us second chances.

EXAMINE THE TEXT

JONAH 3:1-10

The Bible is full of many unusual stories, but the book of Jonah definitely tells one of the most unusual ones! God told a man from Israel named Jonah to go to a place called Nineveh to warn them that they would be destroyed because of their disobedience. Jonah understood this was an opportunity for repentance, so he did not want to go because he did not want the Ninevites to repent.

Nineveh was an enemy to Israel. Jonah did not want to encourage them to repent because he wanted God to destroy them. He might have also been afraid because the Ninevites were a frightening group. What do you think Jonah did? He ran away! He probably thought God would send someone else if he went far enough, so he got on a ship and sailed in the opposite direction. God sent a storm, and when the crew on the ship discovered it was Jonah's fault, they threw him into the sea.

If you do not think this story is already interesting enough, you will want to pay attention to what happened next. God sent a big fish to swallow Jonah, and he had to stay inside the fish for three days. Do you know what Jonah did while he was inside the fish? He prayed.

MEMORY VERSE

JONAH 3:9
Who knows? God may turn and relent; he may turn from his burning anger so that we will not perish.

JONAH

God's plan will be accomplished no matter what we do (Jonah 3:1).

God is merciful to give people second chances to obey (Jonah 3:1).

We can repent and ask God for mercy when we disobey (Jonah 3:10).

God caused the fish to vomit Jonah out on dry land, and in Jonah 3:1–10, God again told Jonah to go to Nineveh. This time Jonah went! He walked through Nineveh warning the people of God's judgment. Just like Jonah feared, the people of Nineveh repented and believed in God. They fasted and called out to God in repentance. God had mercy on them, and everyone was happy. Well, almost everyone was happy.

Jonah did not like that the Ninevites were not destroyed. He went outside the city and sat where he could watch and wait, hoping he would see God punish them anyway. God caused a plant to grow and give Jonah shade, but then He sent a scorching wind and a worm to eat the plant, which left Jonah very uncomfortable. Jonah was upset about losing the plant. God pointed out to Jonah that he did not want a plant destroyed yet he was hoping for the destruction of an entire city full of people.

Wow! There is so much we can learn from Jonah's story. Look at the verses you read earlier to see just a couple of important lessons from his example. Notice that the Lord gave Jonah a second chance to obey. God is merciful. The people believed God and cried out to Him. They did not know if God would still destroy them. They could only ask for mercy and trust His decision. If you have failed to obey God in the past, you can ask for forgiveness. He might give you mercy and a second chance too!

BIG FISH

The blue whale is the largest animal to ever exist. Many people believe that the big fish that swallowed Jonah was a whale.

PRAYER

The story of Jonah is entertaining, but it is also full of helpful examples. When you think of all that God wants to show you through the book of Jonah, thank Him for being a merciful God who gives second chances. Like Jonah, you can recognize ways you have disobeyed God, then you can ask Him to forgive you and help you obey Him better in the future.

NAHUM

PUNISHMENT OR PROTECTION

TEXT TRUTH

God is strong and has authority above all things.

MEMORY VERSE

NAHUM 1:7
The LORD is good, a stronghold in a day of distress; he cares for those who take refuge in him.

EXAMINE THE TEXT

NAHUM 1:5-7

Do you remember what happened with Jonah and the city of Nineveh? In case you forgot, here is the basic story. God told Jonah to go to Nineveh to give them a message. After some disobedience and a few days inside a big fish, Jonah went. The message was a warning, and the people of Nineveh realized they were in a lot of trouble. They repented and asked God for mercy. God decided not to destroy them, and everyone moved on with life.

Sadly, that is not the end of the story for Nineveh. The people of Nineveh did not remain committed to God. Over time they began to do all the terrible things they had done before. Nineveh was a large and strong city. The people enjoyed overpowering others in cruel ways. They earned the coming punishment from God. Even though God had used Nineveh to correct Israel and show His authority, the time had come for judgment. Nahum warned that God's judgment was coming and He was going to destroy the city.

It might seem like the most important part of Nineveh's story is that it was first spared and later destroyed. Actually, the most important part is that God has authority over all things. We can see in Nahum 1:5–7 that God has power over all things. If He is strong enough to cause the mountains to move, He can certainly decide what to do with a rebellious city.

God has authority over everything and everyone in this world. Even though no one and nothing can endure His judgment, you might have noticed in verse 7 that there is something more about God's power. Yes, God is able to send judgment without resistance, but He is also able to protect without resistance. That means people who oppose God have no place to hide from His wrath, and people who love God have nothing to fear. He is stronger than all other things.

FIERCE WARRIORS

How bad were the Assyrians? Nineveh was a capital of the Assyrians, and Nahum called it a bloody, deceitful, warlike city with horses, chariots, and dead bodies everywhere. The Assyrians would do especially awful and cruel things to the people they captured just so other nations would be afraid of them! This stone carving shows an Assyrian soldier fighting a lion with his bare hands! It's no wonder Jonah didn't want to travel to Nineveh! But God told Jonah to go; and once he obeyed, God protected Jonah and used him to spread God's message.

NAHUM

God has authority over all things (Nahum 1:5).

Nothing is more powerful than God (Nahum 1:6).

Nothing can interfere with God's judgment or protection (Nahum 1:6-7).

There is something else in verse 7 that is very important: God knows. He knows who rebels against Him and who loves and obeys Him. God is not going to be fooled by people pretending to repent and obey. He knows exactly what our motives are and what our intentions are.

You can turn from your sin and take refuge in Him. You can ask God for forgiveness and not be like the Ninevites, who only turned to God to be rescued but then turned right back to sin. You can be truly committed to Him. If you love God and have genuine faith in Him, you will be safe from His judgment. Rest in the protection of the one who has more strength and power than all other things.

PRAYER

The Ninevites saw the mercy of God but turned back to their sin. They rebelled and brought judgment on themselves. It is sad that they did not appreciate what they already knew about God. You can thank the Lord that we can learn from the Ninevites, and thank Him for showing us their error so that we can avoid making the same mistake. Ask God to help you love, trust, and obey Him.

JOEL
THE DAY OF THE LORD

TEXT TRUTH

God's judgment of sin is very serious, but He is merciful to allow repentance before it is too late.

EXAMINE THE TEXT

JOEL 2:12-13

The book of Joel tells of things in history about Israel and Judah that also describe things in the future that affect all of us. The Day of the Lord is talked about over and over throughout the book. The Day of the Lord is a way to describe the ultimate expression of God's judgment. His full power and authority will be revealed in a way that settles all questions and doubts about who is in charge. It will be the resolution to what people deserve for their rebellion or devotion to God. That is serious.

We already know that God is patient. He forgives. He has mercy. He gives people second chances.

It can be easy to forget that the same God who does all of that also punishes. The book of Joel reminds us that God takes sin very seriously.

The beginning of Joel describes the results of a drought and locust plague. The land was devastated. There was no water, no wheat, no fruit, nor any other resource. The situation was a problem for everyone. This description helps us imagine the devastation when all is lost. It shows the consequences of sin and desperation for God.

MEMORY VERSE

JOEL 2:13

Tear your hearts, not just your clothes, and return to the LORD your God. For he is gracious and compassionate, slow to anger, abounding in faithful love, and he relents from sending disaster.

JOEL

God's ultimate judgment of sin will be terrible for those who do not repent (Joel 2:11).

God is merciful to offer the opportunity to repent (Joel 2:13).

God wants people's devotion, not just the appearance of obedience (Joel 2:13).

This story is not about locusts. It is about God's judgment. The locusts only show a terrible circumstance. The warning of Joel is not to beware of locusts. It is a warning that God is more powerful than a plague of locusts.

Thankfully, the warning has purpose. It not only reminds us of God's authority to bring judgment, it also reminds us that He offers the opportunity to repent. Joel 2:12–13 shows that in the middle of a terrible warning about punishment and destruction, God allows repentance. He is a very merciful God!

He wants true repentance, not a desperate attempt to escape trouble. It might be tempting to repent out of fear of judgment, but that is not what God wants. He wants you to repent because you recognize His authority as God and you want to live for Him. In verse 13, He tells people to offer their hearts, not their garments. That means He wants people to be truly devoted to Him. He does not want people to only appear to follow Him.

It can be uncomfortable to admit that we need the warnings of God's judgment, but this message from the book of Joel is important for us to know. Sin is a serious problem that requires serious punishment. God is kind to warn us of the consequences of sin because He is the solution to the problem of sin. He will rescue those who repent and have faith. He forgives and saves.

THE LOCUST

Locust swarms have caused trouble for thousands of years. An approaching swarm looks like a big black cloud. As the swarm descends, the insects eat everything in sight. In His warning to Joel, God used locusts as a symbol for destruction.

PRAYER

If you think of all that you have learned so far about the Lord, you will probably have an idea of how He responds to sin and how He responds to repentance. You can talk to God about what He wants for and from your life. You can ask Him to help you be truly devoted to Him and not just appear to follow Him with outward behaviors. You can thank Him for His mercy to warn us of sin's consequences and offer the opportunity to repent.

ROMANS

GOD'S GRACE

TEXT TRUTH

Salvation comes from God as a gift of grace to redeem sinners through the righteousness of Christ.

MEMORY VERSE

ROMANS 3:24
They are justified freely by his grace through the redemption that is in Christ Jesus.

EXAMINE THE TEXT

ROMANS 3:23-24; 6:23

Sometimes we will read things in the Bible that are difficult to think about. They might make us feel uncomfortable, but everything in the Bible matters. What we read in Romans 3:23–24 is very important. In addition to knowing who God is, it is the most important thing we can learn from the Bible. Taking time to think about what the verses mean is a good idea. The passage begins with a problem—sin—and ends with the solution—forgiveness.

If you recognize these verses, you might already know that we all fall short of God's glorious standard. God's standard is perfection, but we do not meet that standard because we have been corrupted by sin. No matter what we do, we are still sinners. Sin cannot be wiped clean. It cannot be erased by good behavior. That is a serious problem because sin has a permanent consequence. We can see that consequence in Romans 6:23. The price of sin is death, but it means more than physical death. It means being separated from God forever.

Our sin requires punishment.

Caesarea Maritima was a place of rule for Roman officials in Paul's time. Paul had to plead his case before the officials and was judged here.

Because God is perfect, He will punish every sin. It would not be consistent for Him to overlook some and punish others, so all sinners must pay the price. That is very bad news because we all sin, so we all deserve to be separated from God.

Thankfully, those verses do not end with the bad news. There is more to know! Romans 3:24 says that God offers the gift of His grace. He is offering something that He knows we do not deserve. We are justified by that grace, which means that even though we are guilty, He will declare us not guilty.

God does not overlook sin. Instead, Jesus is a substitute in our place. When Jesus died on the cross to pay for sin, He took our guilt and gave us His innocence. Through Jesus' sacrifice, the wages of sin were paid and forgiveness is available. Romans 6:23 tells us about God's gift. Although sin brings death, God offers eternal life. So instead of being separated from God forever, we can be with Him forever. What an amazing gift!

ROMANS

We are all sinners who deserve eternal separation from God (Romans 3:23).

God offers the gift of His grace through Jesus (Romans 3:24).

By God's grace through faith in Jesus, we can be forgiven and have eternal life (Romans 6:23).

It is very loving of God to offer a way for sinners to be forgiven. You can keep reading the book of Romans to understand more about salvation. When you think of everything you have learned so far about God's willingness to forgive sinners, you might want to think of what it means for your life and how God graciously wants to save you. You can turn away from sin and trust Jesus in faith.

PRAYER

When you think of what God is showing you as you study the Bible, you might want to ask Him to help you understand the book of Romans and what His grace means for your life. We can all be thankful that Jesus died on the cross to pay for sin. You can ask the Lord to help you recognize your need for Jesus and to help you turn away from sin and trust Him.

PROVERBS

WISDOM IS IN THE WORD

TEXT TRUTH

We can seek wisdom from the Lord by reading His Word.

EXAMINE THE TEXT

PROVERBS 2:1-15

Before you look at the wisdom in the book of Proverbs, there is something very important to know. There are three different ways that God is described in the Bible. He is God the Father, God the Son, and God the Holy Spirit. There is only one God. The Father, Son, and Holy Spirit are three persons of God. That can be confusing because there is nothing anywhere in our lives that compares to God. He is unique. Although the Father, Son, and Holy Spirit are all one, they perform different roles. As you focus on the book of Proverbs, it will help to know a little about the Holy Spirit.

After Jesus' resurrection, He ascended to heaven and sent the Holy Spirit to us. Because of the Holy Spirit, we can have God with us as we go through our daily lives. He comforts us and guides us. One of the most important things the Holy Spirit does for us is help us understand the Bible. Even though anyone can learn the things the Bible teaches, the Holy Spirit helps us understand it the way God intends. We begin to know God better through His Word. We see what it means for our lives and how much God has done for us.

MEMORY VERSE

PROVERBS 2:6
The LORD gives wisdom; from his mouth come knowledge and understanding.

PROVERBS

Along with helping us understand the Bible, the Holy Spirit also helps us apply what we learn from the Bible. Because the Holy Spirit helps us understand and apply God's Word, we are able to gain more wisdom. That is mainly what the book of Proverbs is about—wisdom.

If you look through the pages of Proverbs, it might seem like random advice, but it is actually thorough teaching about right and wrong. It helps us recognize what is wise and what is foolish. To see that for yourself, you can read Proverbs 12:17, 19, 22; 14:5, 25; 19:1.

When you read those verses, you were probably able to see that they all compared the truth with lies. These verses show us that, according to the book of Proverbs, speaking the truth is wise but telling lies is foolish.

Reading through those verses gives you an idea of what to expect when you read through the entire book. Proverbs 2:1–6 shows how we should think about what is in this important book. These verses tell us to be attentive, call out for insight, and much more. Most importantly, they tell us that we can gain wisdom from God. Wisdom is a gift from God. If we depend on the Holy Spirit and the Word of God, we can have the wisdom God offers.

PRAYER

We can have wisdom from God through the Bible and the Holy Spirit. When you thank God for giving you the opportunity to gain wisdom, you can ask Him to help you understand and apply the things you learn from the Bible. God understands if you have trouble reading the Bible. You can turn to Him when you need help or guidance. He will show you the important things He wants you to know. He will also give you wisdom.

HOLY SPIRIT

The Holy Spirit helps us to understand the Bible and to be wise so that we can live in God's will. We can't see the Holy Spirit, but in Matthew 3:13-17, the Holy Spirit descended on Jesus in the form of a dove while Jesus was being baptized by John the Baptist.

SONG OF SONGS
THE LOVE OF LOVES

TEXT TRUTH

There is no love greater than God's perfect love for us.

EXAMINE THE TEXT

SONG OF SONGS 2:11-12

Have you ever read that Jesus is the King of kings? It is a name for Jesus that describes Him as the King over all other kings. You might say He is the top King or the best King. That is the idea for the title of the book of Song of Songs. It is like saying this is the best song. More specifically, this is the best of Solomon's songs. This book is a very poetic description of love. It emphasizes the beauty of God-honoring love.

Song of Songs 2:11–12 uses the changing season to describe a couple's growing love for each other and how they are looking forward to spending more time together. You might be asking yourself how poetry about love can help us know anything about God. The truth is, you will probably understand this book better when you are older, but you can already understand love. You can probably think of many different people in your life who love you. Consider all the

MEMORY VERSE

SONG OF SONGS 2:12

The blossoms appear in the countryside. The time of singing has come, and the turtledove's cooing is heard in our land.

different types of relationships, such as parents, siblings, cousins, friends, and so on. Those relationships can help you understand God's love better. God's love is the best love. We can say that His love is the love of loves!

When you read 1 Corinthians 13:4–7 you will see a straightforward description of love in its perfect form. It includes patience, kindness, self-lessness, and hope. It is our example as the standard of love. Only one person has ever perfectly exhibited that standard of love—Jesus.

CHANGING SEASONS

The Song of Songs is a work of poetry by King Solomon. He used symbolism such as the image of blossoming trees as the seasons change to describe the growth of love.

SONG OF SONGS

KEY POINTS

Jesus is the perfect example of love (1 John 3:16).

When Jesus came to earth, He arrived for one purpose. He came to die on a cross to pay the penalty of sin. He never sinned, so He did not deserve the punishment of death. He loved us enough to die anyway. His sacrifice made it possible for us to be forgiven of our sins. That is perfect love.

PRAYER

You can learn about God's love from the different relationships you have in your life. Ask God to help you follow His example and love others. You can thank God for all the people in your life who love you, and thank Him for the opportunity to love them as well. You can also ask God to help you love Him more and to recognize His love for you.

LUKE

BE HUMBLE LIKE JESUS

TEXT TRUTH

Jesus taught humility by how He served others and treated people with kindness.

EXAMINE THE TEXT

LUKE 22:24-27

When Jesus was on the earth, He spent a period of time carefully teaching twelve specific men. Jesus chose to give them personal instruction and guidance to prepare them to carry His message to others after His return to heaven. These special friends were ordinary men with different lifestyles and experiences. They got to see firsthand how Jesus treated everyone equally. However, they sometimes still expected some people to be greater than others. That is what they debated after their last Passover meal with Jesus.

You can see how Jesus corrected them in Luke 22:24–27, especially verse 27. Imagine what was happening. This was the same meal where Jesus served them the bread and the cup in expectation of His death on the cross. He was focused on much more important things. We know from the book of John that this was also the occasion when Jesus washed the men's feet. Jesus was not simply telling them to be humble; He was also showing them how!

MEMORY VERSE

LUKE 22:27

"Who is greater, the one at the table or the one serving? Isn't it the one at the table? But I am among you as the one who serves."

LUKE

Jesus corrected the disciples when they argued about which of them was greater (Luke 22:26).

We should follow Jesus' example of humility (Luke 22:26-27).

Instead of demanding to be served, Jesus served others (Luke 22:27).

In verse 27, Jesus asked an obvious question about which person is greater, the one serving or the one being served. It is easy to assume that the person being served is greater. That is why it is so important to realize that Jesus was serving them. Jesus came to earth to serve others. No one is greater than Jesus. So we cannot measure greatness by who gets treated better or by any other-worldly standard. Our example of greatness is Jesus. The Lord of all creation came to earth. That alone is amazing! He could have demanded anything. After all, He is God. Instead, He washed feet, healed diseases, helped the poor, and died for sinners.

When you read the stories about Jesus in the Bible, you will learn that He reached out to people who were not accepted in society. He touched people who had been avoided by everyone else. He talked to people whom others considered unworthy. He forgave liars and thieves and immoral people. There was not a person who came in contact with Him who was greater than Him in any way. Yet He was kind and compassionate. Even though He knew of His own greatness and that everyone He encountered owed Him worship and reverence, He still humbled Himself to serve them.

We can learn so much from Jesus' willingness to serve others. He showed us that no one is greater than anyone else, and we should not compare ourselves or try to measure greatness. Instead, we should follow His example by being compassionate and respectful to everyone. That begins with humility. Jesus humbled Himself when He came to earth. He humbled Himself when He washed the disciples' feet. He humbled Himself when He died on the cross. Because of Him we know how to be kind and humble. You can follow the example of Jesus by being kind and serving others.

PRAYER

Jesus humbled Himself while He was on earth. He treated people with respect and kindness in a way that is an example to us. You can thank God for giving us the example of how we should treat others, and ask Him to help you be humble and kind. You can also ask God to show you if there are ways that you are not being respectful to people and ask Him to help you correct those behaviors.

This basin is almost 2,800 years old! The basin was filled with water, and a person's foot was placed in the center to be washed. Jesus might have used something similar to this to wash His disciples' feet. It was a very special way for Jesus to show His followers the importance of serving others.

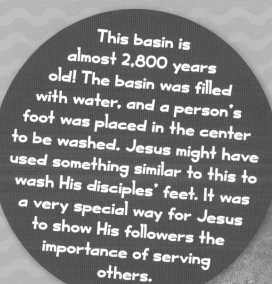

SERVE OTHERS

EPHESIANS
LIVE FOR GOD

TEXT TRUTH

One of the most important ways we can live for God is to treat others well.

EXAMINE THE TEXT

EPHESIANS 2:8-10; 4:1-3, 32

It is only fair to warn you that these verses are going to challenge you to live for God. Hopefully you will be excited about what you read, because they are very encouraging verses. You can see that for yourself beginning with Ephesians 2:8–10. Those verses free us from ever worrying about whether we are doing enough for God to save us. We cannot do enough for Him to save us. People are not saved by what they do. Only God saves. We can see in verse 8 that He saves by grace through faith. What a relief! Salvation is not up to us, so we cannot fail. We are only expected to trust God, and He never fails.

We already know that good works do not save us, so there is another purpose for the good works mentioned in verse 10. When you read Ephesians 4:1–3, you will see that along with giving us examples of how we should live, these verses also tell us why. You probably noticed in the first verse that we are to live in a worthy manner. That means those who are saved are to live in a way that is worthy of what God has done. Good works do not save, but they do honor God.

MEMORY VERSE

EPHESIANS 2:10

We are his workmanship, created in Christ Jesus for good works, which God prepared ahead of time for us to do.

THE GIFT

The Bible tells us that salvation is a gift from God. Read Ephesians 2:8-9 to see what is said about this special gift. Have you received this gift yet?

God does not want or need us to repay Him for the gift of salvation. He only wants us to make the most of it. He wants us to live in ways that honor Him. God gives our lives purpose. If you look again at the second verse, you can see examples of how we can do that.

One of the most important ways we can live a life worthy of salvation is to treat others well. We can see that in Ephesians 4:32. Jesus is our motivation and our example. He wants us to be humble and patient and forgiving. The way we treat others is more than a kind act. It can also be an act of worship. When we follow the instruction of the Bible to honor God, that is a part of worship.

You can probably imagine many different ways to express kindness to others. Whether you are with a close friend or someone you do not like being around at all, there will

EPHESIANS

You cannot live for God to gain salvation, but you can live for God because of salvation (Ephesians 2:9-10).

KEY POINTS

Make every effort to live for God (Ephesians 4:1).

always be ways to show patience and humility. You can be selfless and considerate even to people who do not treat you with the same kindness. No matter whom you encounter, you always have the opportunity to live for God by the way you treat them. Honor God in everything you do.

One way to live for God is to be kind to others (Ephesians 4:32).

PRAYER

There are many things the Bible tells us to think of as we live for God. When you think of what God showed you today, ask Him to help you apply those lessons in your life. You can also ask Him to help you want the same things He wants for your life. Thank God for giving you purpose and for making a way for you to live with Him forever.

NUMBERS
TRUST GOD

EXAMINE THE TEXT

NUMBERS 14:19-24; 26:64-65

Did you know that Moses used spies? It is true! God had him send spies to find out information about Canaan, the land that God had promised to give the Israelites. There were twelve spies selected; one from each tribe of Israel. The spies spent forty days gathering information. When they returned to give a report of what they had seen, they told of all the great things available in the land, but they also mentioned that the cities looked large and difficult to enter. Not only that, but they also told how the people seemed tall and strong.

Their report really frightened the Israelites, so they did not want to try to go take the land. That was a problem because God had already promised the land to them. It should not have mattered what the spies saw; they should have known they could conquer anything with God on their side. Sadly, they did not use the information to take over Canaan. Instead, they used it as an excuse to stay out!

Ten of the spies were afraid of the people of Canaan and their own people, so they argued against going. But two of them, Caleb and Joshua, realized that this was not about the strength of the cities or the people.

MEMORY VERSE

NUMBERS 14:21
As surely as I live and as the whole earth is filled with the LORD's glory.

NUMBERS

KEY POINTS

We can trust God to keep His promises (Numbers 14:30, 38).

There are consequences for disobeying God (Numbers 26:65).

We should trust God even when others do not (Numbers 14:24).

It was about God. They remembered that God had promised that land to them. They knew that if they trusted God they would be all right no matter what. The two men tried to get the people to trust God, but it did not work.

God was not happy. Actually, God was so unhappy that He even offered to get rid of all of the Israelites and give Moses an entirely new and better group! You can read Numbers 14:19 to see how Moses responded to that offer by asking God to pardon them! He appealed to God for mercy.

If you keep reading verses 20–24, you will see that God did not start over with a new group of Israelites, so that was merciful, but He did have a consequence for the rebellious group. All the people who had argued against taking over Canaan were never going to be allowed to go in. There were only two people who trusted God. That is astonishing, because there were hundreds of thousands of Israelites!

It was probably not easy for Caleb and Joshua to stand up for God when the people around them rebelled. There might be times in your life when you have to make a similar decision. You might be alone and afraid and unsure about something that seems impossible. In those times, you can remember Joshua and Caleb and always trust God.

Ancient Jericho is likely the oldest city ever found! Some of these ancient ruins are from the time of Joshua. In the ruins, you can see the base of an old tower where people may have kept watch for spies. Jericho was an important city long before Joshua and the Israelites conquered it.

PRAYER

When you think about what you learned from the Bible about trusting God, you can ask the Lord to help you trust Him in every circumstance, even if everyone else around you is too afraid. You can thank God for being trustworthy and ask Him to give you the courage to trust Him if you are ever afraid of what He wants you to do. You can also ask God to have mercy and forgive you any time you fail to trust Him.

DEUTERONOMY
LOVE AND OBEY

TEXT TRUTH

We are to love God completely and obey Him in every situation.

EXAMINE THE TEXT

DEUTERONOMY 6:4-5

Just like the rest of the Bible, the book of Deuteronomy has a lot for us to learn about God and how to live for Him. The book of Deuteronomy shares two main lessons Moses wanted people to remember. So you will see as you read Deuteronomy that people are to love and obey God. Throughout the entire book Moses gives instructions to love God and obey Him.

It is important for us to know what was happening when Moses gave these instructions. Soon he was going to be replaced by Joshua, and Deuteronomy records the final speeches of Moses before that transition. Those speeches included a summary of the history of the Israelites, the commands God had given, encouragement to repent, and so much more. Moses knew that the people of Israel would have a much different experience if they avoided their old pattern of sin and did things God's way.

That was true for the Israelites, and it is true for all of us. If we love and obey Him, we should want to follow all of God's commands. Those very simple instructions that we read in Deuteronomy

MEMORY VERSE

DEUTERONOMY 6:5
Love the LORD your God with all your heart, with all your soul, and with all your strength.

6:4–5 affect every part of life. No one else deserves our love and obedience. There is only one God, and He is the only one worthy of our devotion, which is exactly what God wants. He wants us to love Him completely.

Loving God includes obeying Him too. We truly love God when we do things His way in every part of life. Those two simple instructions to love and obey might not seem as simple once we think of all the things God desires from us. The truth is, we all struggle to love God the way we should. The only one who has ever accomplished that perfectly was Jesus. So He is our perfect example to follow.

When you notice that you are not living for God the way He commands, you can talk to Him. You can ask God to help you love Him and obey Him.

ANCIENT LAWS

The Ur-Nammu Law Code is the oldest known law from people called the Sumerians over 4,000 years ago!

DEUTERONOMY

Moses instructed us to love and obey God (Deuteronomy 6:5).

We are commanded to love God completely (Deuteronomy 6:5).

The command to love God is a command to live for Him (Deuteronomy 6:5).

God deserves our love and obedience (Deuteronomy 6:4).

Taking your needs to God in prayer is a very special way to love and obey Him. When you think back over all that you have learned about the struggles of the Israelites, you can remember what their example has taught you about God. You know that He is patient, forgiving, faithful, and worthy. Knowing that will help you love and obey God completely.

PRAYER

God wants you to honor Him by obeying Him in daily life. When you think of what the Lord is teaching you from the Bible, you might want to thank Him for letting you know who He is and that He deserves to be obeyed. You can also ask God to give you love for Him and excitement to keep His commands.

JOB

TRUST GOD ANYHOW

TEXT TRUTH

Even when we do not understand why things happen, we can still trust God.

EXAMINE THE TEXT

JOB 1:22; 2:10; 19:25

In case you have never read the book of Job, you need to be warned. Job had some problems. You see, God allowed Satan to test Job. God knew that Job was devoted to Him, but

MEMORY VERSE

JOB 19:25

I know that my Redeemer lives, and at the end he will stand on the dust.

Satan wanted to prove that he could cause Job to turn away from God. He claimed that Job only followed God because he was comfortable and wealthy. He was right about one thing. Job did have a prosperous life. Not only did he have excessive wealth, but he also had seven sons and three daughters.

Job's five hundred oxen and five hundred donkeys were stolen after many of his servants who had apparently been caring for his animals were killed. While the messenger who was telling Job about his oxen, donkeys, and servants was still speaking, another messenger arrived with a new problem. Job's seven thousand sheep and the servants caring for them had been consumed by a fire. While that messenger was talking, another messenger arrived with yet another problem. Job's three thousand camels had been stolen after the servants caring for them were killed. That means all of Job's animals and servants were gone.

JOB

Even when he lost everything, Job still hoped in God (Job 19:25).

KEY POINTS

We can trust God even when we suffer (Job 2:10).

We can trust God even when we do not understand why something is happening (Job 2:10).

When you read Job 1:22, you will see that Job did not respond the way Satan thought he would. However, unfortunately, there was much more to come. While the messenger who was telling Job about his camels and servants was still speaking, another messenger arrived with even more devastating news. This messenger told Job that his sons and daughters had been celebrating together when the house fell and killed them all. What a horrible, horrible day that must have been for Job!

There was one final problem that Satan inflicted on Job. When Satan realized that taking things from Job would not be enough to turn him away from God, he decided to ruin Job's health. He was sure that inflicting Job with painful sores all over his body would certainly turn him from God.

Job 2:10 shows that, again, Job did not respond the way Satan thought he would. Of course, this was not easy for Job. Most of the book is dedicated to his anguish as he struggled to understand his loss. In fact, many times he responded in sinful ways. Still, he trusted God.

At one point, after one of his friends tried to convince him that his suffering was some sort of punishment for his sins, Job made a confident statement that we can all take comfort in. This statement, from Job 19:25, shows the depths of his trust in God.

Nothing about Job's situation made sense to him, and there seemed to be no relief, but he knew God was still in control and that no matter what happened in his life, God would still be God. You can think of Job when you face challenges in life to remember that we can trust God no matter what.

GOD SPEAKS

PRAYER

Even though Job's struggles were unusual, we will all face difficult times in life. You can thank the Lord for giving us Job's example and ask for help to remain focused on Him during times of difficulty. You can trust God as your Redeemer and have faith in His plan, even when you do not understand it. You can ask Him to help you remember that He will always be with you.

Job was a wealthy and respected man who faithfully followed God. Satan tested Job by taking away everything Job had and by causing a lot of pain, sickness, and suffering in his life. This confused Job and made him ask God many questions. God spoke to Job through a whirlwind and helped him to have faith.

ECCLESIASTES
EMPTY WITHOUT GOD

TEXT TRUTH

If we live for God, He will bring eternal purpose to everything we do in life.

EXAMINE THE TEXT

ECCLESIASTES 1:1-9; 2:25-26

Have you ever had anyone give you news that you thought at first was really terrible, then as you learned more, you realized it was actually great news? That is similar to what happens in the book of Ecclesiastes. It begins with some very discouraging points made by King Solomon, but then we see that there is more to the story.

When you read through the book of Ecclesiastes, you will notice that Solomon repeated a word many times. Depending on the translation of the Bible you are using, it might be *vanity* or *futility* or some other similar word. He used that word to describe things as pointless or temporary or worthless.

MEMORY VERSE

ECCLESIASTES 2:25
Who can eat and who can enjoy life apart from him?

When you read Ecclesiastes 1:1–9, you will see right away that Solomon described everything as pointless. Those verses seem discouraging. Generations come and go, the wind keeps going around, and the streams flow in and out of the sea. Things just continue without completion in repetitive circles for no apparent reason. Solomon wanted to show that nothing really has a purpose.

Have you ever earned something that you worked really hard for? Maybe you studied to get a good grade or you trained hard to finish a race. According to Solomon, that time was wasted because soon there will be another grade or another race. Do you agree that it was a waste of time? Hopefully not because there is more to Solomon's message.

When you read the entire book, you will notice that working and living wisely are both futile, along with wealth and honor. However, there is something especially troubling in the second chapter. According to Solomon, laughter and enjoyment have no value. He was a wealthy king. He was able to test this theory thoroughly by indulging in every possible luxury, but he realized that entertainment was completely worthless.

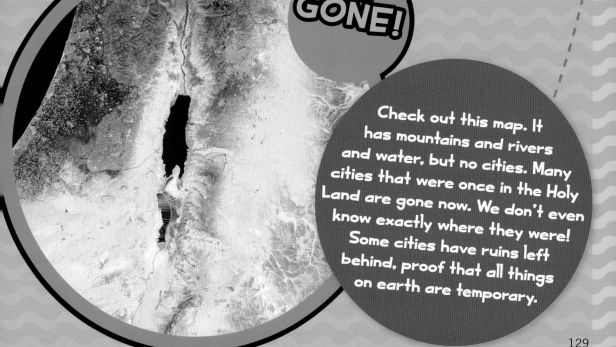

ALL GONE!

Check out this map. It has mountains and rivers and water, but no cities. Many cities that were once in the Holy Land are gone now. We don't even know exactly where they were! Some cities have ruins left behind, proof that all things on earth are temporary.

ECCLESIASTES

Wow. This book does not seem like a lot of fun. It is a good thing that Solomon did not stop with these conclusions because we would have no reason to work hard or learn or enjoy anything. The rest of Solomon's message is in Ecclesiastes 2:25–26: Everything changes when we have God.

It is true that nothing lasts forever, unless you have God. Nothing has purpose, unless it is done for God. Everything will come and go on the earth, but with God there is more than this life. He offers everlasting joy, which is far better than the temporary fun of this world.

So now we know the full message. The book of Ecclesiastes was not written to tell us that nothing matters. It was written to tell us that nothing matters without God. If we live for Him, everything matters. The ordinary or repetitive or difficult or outrageously fun things in life are either going to blow away with time or they are going to honor God forever.

PRAYER

The Lord gives us many things that we can do every day to serve Him. There is nothing in life that is meaningless when we live for God. You can thank God for giving your life purpose and ask Him to help you understand how to live for Him. You can ask God to help you fill your days with things that He wants in your life. You can also thank Him for showing you that He gives your life eternal purpose.

ISAIAH

WHO WILL GO?

TEXT TRUTH

We should be willing to do whatever God wants us to do and go wherever He wants us to go.

EXAMINE THE TEXT

ISAIAH 6:8

There are several books in the Bible that explain specific messages God gave through some of His prophets. Prophets were chosen by God and given direct messages from Him to share with people. You might remember that there are books of the Minor Prophets and books of the Major Prophets. The books of the Major Prophets are not more important. They are just longer, so God must have given those prophets more to say! One of the books of the Major Prophets is Isaiah. Isaiah had a very willing attitude to serve God and an eagerness to share His message, even when he did not know what to expect.

There was always hope in God's messages because He offered forgiveness and mercy. In fact, that was the ultimate message of all of the prophets. However, many of the things the prophets were tasked with telling people began with terrible warnings. In Isaiah's situation, the people had become corrupt and were not truly worshiping God. They followed proper religious practices, but they were not loyal to the Lord. So no matter how faithful they were to the law, it did not matter because they were not faithful to God.

MEMORY VERSE

ISAIAH 6:8
I heard the voice of the Lord asking: Who should I send? Who will go for us? I said: Here I am. Send me.

ISAIAH

Isaiah was willing to obey God even before knowing what would be expected of him (Isaiah 6:8).

Isaiah got to be a very special messenger for God (Isaiah 9:6).

Obedience to God can impact the world for many generations (Isaiah 51:8).

Isaiah was faithful to God. He worshiped God and nothing else. Not only that, but he was ready to obey when God had something for him to do. We can see that in his response to God in Isaiah 6:8. The people of Israel were in such rebellion that they needed urgent warnings to repent, yet Isaiah eagerly surrendered to whatever God had planned for him. He agreed to go wherever God wanted him to go without knowing what to expect. He fully trusted God.

The things we can learn from Isaiah's situation are useful in our lives today. There are still people who follow the rules and participate in church who are not truly devoted to God. They think that if they do all the right things they will get credit for obeying. That is not how it works. God does not want empty actions. He wants worship.

Because Isaiah obeyed God, he was able to be a part of something very special. Not only did he give the messages to the Israelites, which are still helpful today, but he also got to tell people about Jesus! Being able to share this message was a very special privilege for Isaiah. Remember, Jesus had not even been born yet! God was allowing Isaiah to describe things that would happen hundreds of years later. What an amazing opportunity!

When God gives you the chance to do something for Him, you will certainly want to do it. You never know what He will allow you to be a part of. Isaiah's message is still helpful today. His words have endured for many generations and still point people to Jesus. You can follow Isaiah's example and be ready to go wherever God leads. You will definitely be a part of something special that God is doing in the world, and you will get to point people to Jesus!

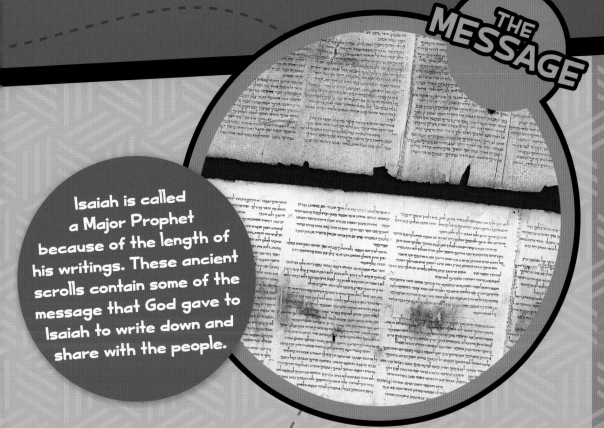

Isaiah is called a Major Prophet because of the length of his writings. These ancient scrolls contain some of the message that God gave to Isaiah to write down and share with the people.

PRAYER

We know from Isaiah's example that if we trust God, He will use us in ways that affect the world. You can thank God for giving you the opportunity to obey Him and talk to Him about the difficulties or distractions that keep you from doing what He wants you to do. You can also ask God to give you the courage to trust Him even before you know what He will ask of you.

MICAH

DEVOTION, NOT DUTY

TEXT TRUTH

God wants people to serve Him out of love and devotion.

MEMORY VERSE

MICAH 6:8
Mankind, he has told each of you what is good and what it is the LORD requires of you: to act justly, to love faithfulness, and to walk humbly with your God.

EXAMINE THE TEXT

MICAH 6:8

Micah was a prophet of God who shared a very similar message to the one Isaiah gave. Even though the book of Micah is much shorter than the book of Isaiah, the message he gave was just as serious and just as important. Micah was responsible for warning the Israelites to stop worshiping other gods and repent or they would be severely punished.

When you read about the different messages to the people of Israel, you might be tempted to think that God never follows through with His warnings to sinners. That is not true. He always follows through. In fact,

Israel faced repeated consequences for their sins. The kingdom of Israel was divided by the time Micah came along, and there was another season of captivity on the way.

God's judgment is serious. He will always punish sin, but He is also patient and merciful. Because of His mercy, God allows people the opportunity to repent. When Micah spoke

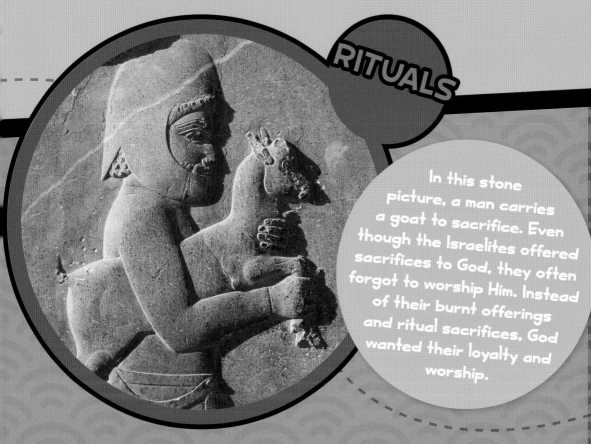

In this stone picture, a man carries a goat to sacrifice. Even though the Israelites offered sacrifices to God, they often forgot to worship Him. Instead of their burnt offerings and ritual sacrifices, God wanted their loyalty and worship.

to the people, he reminded them of how they were rescued from Egypt. They had apparently assumed that their rescue was because of their own worth or as a reward. Instead, Micah reminded them that it was God's grace and mercy that delivered them from captivity. Instead of their insincere offerings and actions, God wanted their loyalty and worship. He wanted them to live for Him.

God was giving examples of how to live for Him. He wanted to make it clear that their rituals were meaningless to Him. He wanted their lives to be driven by worship. He wanted their actions to be a result of their

dedication to Him. You can see when you read Micah 6:8 that God is still wanting the same thing now. He wants that from you.

People make similar mistakes today that the Israelites made. They do things trying to earn God's favor instead of to honor Him. In place of burnt offerings or ritual sacrifices, they do things like go to church or learn a lot of Bible stories to try and appease God. Those are things we should be doing because we love God.

It is very good to go to church and learn the Bible. Those are opportunities God gives us to know Him and serve Him. The problem is that sometimes

MICAH

KEY POINTS

The Israelites were not serving God wholeheartedly (Micah 6:2).

God wants us to serve only Him (Micah 6:8).

God wants our love and devotion (Micah 6:8).

people think that they can get away with sin as long as they go to church too. That is not true worship. When you think of your own life, you might want to ask yourself how you show your love for God and if there are things in your life that you hope God will overlook.

The Israelites wanted to know what they could do that would qualify as enough. They thought there was a specific measurement of how much they could do for God to get by. If you only try to get by or think of service to God as a duty that pays for sin, these are good things to talk about with God. He wants your devotion, not your duty.

God might be showing you these things through the book of Micah to help you recognize that He is patiently giving you the opportunity to repent. He is a patient and loving God. We should all live for Him with humility and kindness.

PRAYER

The Israelites did not follow God out of love and devotion. They only did what they thought would be enough to earn God's favor. God wants more than that. We can thank God for the lessons we are able to learn from the examples in Scripture. You can ask Him to show you what He wants you to do differently in your life because of what you learned from the book of Micah. You can also ask God to help you love Him and serve Him wholeheartedly.

JOHN
THE WAY TO HEAVEN

TEXT TRUTH

There is only one way to heaven, and that is through Jesus Christ the Savior.

EXAMINE THE TEXT

JOHN 14:1-7

There are so many exciting and wonderful things to learn from the book of John. It is a helpful and encouraging book that shows us the love and kindness of Jesus. So many of the stories in John describe Jesus patiently teaching people. He chose disciples to be with Him for a while so that He could spend time giving them more specific instruction and guidance.

During one conversation with His disciples, He attempted to help them prepare for His leaving. He knew that He would only be with them a little longer and they would need to carry on without Him. As He was warning them of coming events, He emphasized something very important that He knew would bring comfort to them in His absence.

MEMORY VERSE

JOHN 14:6

Jesus told him, "I am the way, the truth, and the life. No one comes to the Father except through me."

When you read John 14:1–7, you can see what Jesus told His disciples to give them comfort. Jesus wanted His disciples to know that they would be together again in heaven. The men did not fully understand His words at the time, but Jesus would soon die on a cross. Jesus died to pay the penalty for sin! Jesus lived a perfect life, so He was able to be a substitute for sinners. His death satisfied God's judgment against sin.

137

JOHN

Jesus comforted the disciples by telling them of heaven (John 14:2).

Jesus is the only way to heaven (John 14:6).

We can spend eternity with God because of Jesus (John 3:16).

The disciples did not know the grief and fear that they were about to experience. Jesus did. He knew that His words would help them through their struggles. He also knew that they would be comforting words for us. We do not have to experience the same struggles as the disciples in order to be excited about heaven. Even the best things on earth will not compare to the wonders and glory of heaven. It is almost impossible to imagine what a happy place heaven will be.

The disciples were not clear about what Jesus was describing. They asked Him how to get where He was going. If you look again at verses 6 and 7, you will notice that Jesus told the men that He is the only way to the Father, and knowing Jesus is knowing God. It is exciting to think of being with God forever. We can be with God in perfection for eternity. That sounds pretty great.

Sometimes people are so distracted by the idea of heaven that they forget the greatness of God. They forget what Jesus explained to the disciples.

There is only one way to heaven. Some people would like to get to heaven another way. They think that if we all worship something sincerely enough that we are all moving in the same direction. They misunderstand who Jesus is and what happened when He died on the cross.

You do not have to be confused by any other ideas about heaven. Jesus told us exactly how to get there. He is the only way. Jesus' words were not only for the people who were with Him while He was on earth. They are for you too. You can have faith in Jesus for salvation and eternal life.

PRAYER

God gave us the Bible so that we would know Him. The book of John makes it clear that Jesus is the only way to heaven. You can thank God for the Bible and for Jesus being the way that we can be forgiven and have eternal life. If you ask the Lord to help you have faith in Jesus, you can also ask Him to help you understand everything you need to know about trusting Him and living for Him.

In the book of John, Jesus called Himself the "good shepherd." Tending sheep (shepherding) was usually done by the youngest son, women, or thieves. Shepherding was not a desired job. The sheep needed to be watched and cared for at all times.

1 THESSALONIANS
KEEP ENCOURAGING OTHERS

TEXT TRUTH

We can honor God by obeying the Bible and being an encouragement to others.

EXAMINE THE TEXT

1 THESSALONIANS 5:11

Have you ever been left alone in a situation where you were supposed to follow some instructions? Maybe a teacher left the classroom for a few minutes or a parent allowed you to stay in the backyard. Those situations can help you relate to what was happening with the Thessalonian church. Paul had been there teaching and guiding the people, but he had to leave. There was no established leadership, so the new believers were under a lot of pressure. They had people trying to confuse them and get them to stop believing in Jesus.

The Thessalonians handled the pressure very well. They followed Paul's instructions and stood firm against the problems they faced, even though they had no reason to expect their struggles to go away. Paul tried to get them to focus on what was most important. He reminded them of the reason for their faith and encouraged them to keep living for God.

There were several things that he briefly mentioned to help them stay on course, but one specific verse gives an idea of Paul's message. It is 1 Thessalonians 5:11. He wanted them to continue encouraging one another. That tells us a lot about the Thessalonians, but it also gives us something to apply to our own lives.

MEMORY VERSE

1 THESSALONIANS 5:11
Encourage one another and build each other up as you are already doing.

Paul was commending them for living out the things they had been learning about God. The Thessalonians were building each other up to honor God.

We can look around at the people in our lives and find ways to encourage them. It is an important example of one way we can apply what we are learning from the Bible. God always wants us to be kind and encouraging to others. He loves people and wants everyone to be treated well. If we build others up, we are obeying this verse and honoring God.

It can be different in every circumstance, but building someone up might be as simple as a kind word or a friendly gesture. It can be anything that makes someone feel supported. The people of the Thessalonian church were facing pressure from others outside the church. It was probably helpful to feel like they were not alone. Something as simple as making someone feel supported can be encouraging.

The "Street Called Straight" in Damascus is known as the oldest working road in the world. The road has been modified, but the path would have been used by Saul when he arrived in Damascus. Soon after, he became known as Paul and spent the rest of his life encouraging others to follow Jesus.

1 THESSALONIANS

KEY POINTS

We can honor God by encouraging one another (1 Thessalonians 5:11).

The Thessalonians are a great example for us. They were not perfect people. They had problems understanding some of the things Paul taught. They needed a lot of guidance and instruction. They did not always get it right, but they lived for God. We might not always get it right either, so we can learn from their example and do better as we learn more from the Bible. There are many ways to honor God each and every day. Now, thanks to Paul's letter to the Thessalonians, we know that one way we can honor Him is by building others up and being encouraging.

PRAYER

Paul's letter to the people of the Thessalonian church can be a helpful reminder for us to keep living for God. You can thank the Lord for His Word, for how He gives us instruction through the examples of others, and for the things you are learning that help you obey Him. You can ask Him to help you encourage others as an act of obedience to His Word.

2 THESSALONIANS
LEARN AND LIVE

TEXT TRUTH

We should learn what is true from Scripture and obey it so we will not be distracted or idle.

EXAMINE THE TEXT

2 THESSALONIANS 2:13-17

Paul's second letter to the people in the Thessalonian church will cause us to ask ourselves if we know what is true and if we are actively living for God. You probably remember from the book of 1 Thessalonians that this group was a young church. They had not been believers for very long, and they did not have strong leadership with them all the time.

Paul commended them for handling their struggles against outside resistance so well. He encouraged them to continue living for God and to continue growing in their faith. This letter was sent specifically to address confusion being caused by false teachings about the return of Christ.

MEMORY VERSE

2 THESSALONIANS 2:14
He called you to this through our gospel, so that you might obtain the glory of our Lord Jesus Christ.

After His resurrection, Jesus ascended to heaven. He will come again someday to gather believers and take them to heaven with Him. This was important to the people in that church. They were clinging to that hope because it was a great encouragement. Sadly, some people were telling them that Christ had already returned, and this was a frightening distraction. They were not sure if they understood Paul's teaching, and they were allowing this issue to become disruptive.

2 THESSALONIANS

Study the Bible to learn what is true (2 Thessalonians 2:15).

KEY POINTS

Obey the Bible to stay busy living for God (2 Thessalonians 3:6).

Paul explained some specific things they could expect as signs of Christ's return in order to ease their minds. With better understanding, they could have confidence and not be distracted when others made false claims. That is why 2 Thessalonians encourages us to ask ourselves what is true. If we study the Bible, we will know what is true. If we know God's Word, we are less likely to get distracted by anything else. We can recognize false teachings and avoid confusion.

One of the other things Paul addressed with the people of the Thessalonian church was their laziness. Some in the church had apparently not been active in working and were becoming a burden to others. The charity intended for those in true need had been exhausted by those who were simply unwilling to provide for themselves. Not only were they a drain on their fellow Christian brothers and sisters, but they were also not representing Christ. That is why 2 Thessalonians encourages us to ask ourselves if we are actively living for God.

If we are busy doing what we can for the Lord, we will not get caught up in meaningless activities and other people's business.

The most important thing we can do is apply what we are learning from the Bible. That is the best way to stay active for God, because the things we learn will lead us to better decisions and better management of our time each day.

You might not be confused about the same things as the people who originally read this letter, but you can learn how to focus on God's Word and apply what you are learning. You can have faith in Jesus and live a life that honors Him.

PRAYER

Paul's letter to the people of the Thessalonian church shows us that in order to grow in understanding and obedience we must rely on Scripture. You can talk to God about anything in the Bible that confuses you. He will help you understand what it means and how it applies to your life. When you thank God for giving us examples to learn how to live, you can ask Him to help you live a life that honors Him.

LIVE FOR GOD

This is the traditional home of Simon the tanner, where Peter stayed when God sent him to Joppa. This is an example of people practicing charity by opening their homes to travelers.

1 KINGS

GOD OR BAAL

EXAMINE THE TEXT

1 KINGS 18:21, 38-39

You probably already know that the Israelites were not always obedient to God. In fact, they had been so rebellious that they included other gods in their burnt offerings! That is not the kind of offering God will accept. A prophet named Elijah was sent to tell them messages from God. He made it very clear that they needed to repent and serve only God. On one particular occasion he made a dramatic point about the gods the people were serving.

This story began when God sent a drought to remind the people to follow Him. God also sent Elijah to hide because the prophets of God were in danger. The queen worshiped Baal, a false god. She did not want God's messages being spread, so she ordered that all the prophets be killed. Elijah followed God's instructions and stayed hidden by a brook until the Lord gave him new instructions. He sent Elijah to see King Ahab. Ahab was surprised he had come and called Elijah a troublemaker when he saw him. Elijah was not intimidated and countered that the king was the troublemaker for leading the people to follow false gods. That is when things started to get really exciting!

MEMORY VERSE

1 KINGS 18:39
When all the people saw it, they fell facedown and said, "The LORD, he is God! The LORD, he is God!"

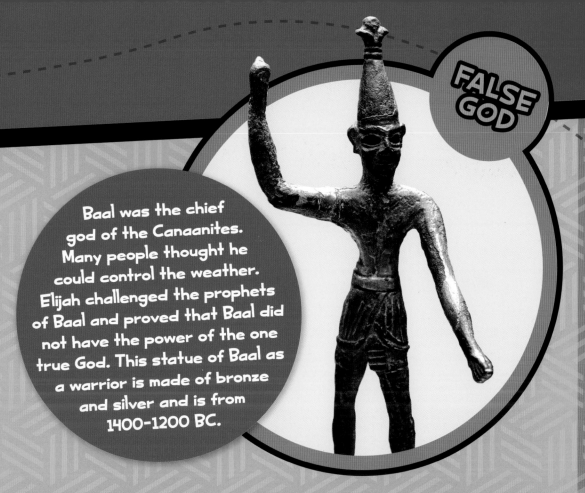

Baal was the chief god of the Canaanites. Many people thought he could control the weather. Elijah challenged the prophets of Baal and proved that Baal did not have the power of the one true God. This statue of Baal as a warrior is made of bronze and silver and is from 1400-1200 BC.

Elijah invited Ahab to gather all the people of Israel and all the prophets of Ahab's gods to meet together at Mount Carmel. Elijah began in 1 Kings 18:21 by challenging the people. He made it clear that they should determine who the real God is. They should not try to worship different gods.

Then Elijah pointed out that he was the only prophet of God present, while Ahab had gathered hundreds of Baal's prophets. Elijah then invited them to select a bull and build an altar to their gods. They would not light a fire. Instead, they would call out to their gods to light the fire for them. That would prove whether their gods had any power.

They selected a bull and built the altar. They cried out for hours, but nothing happened. Then it was Elijah's turn. He built an altar to the Lord with twelve stones representing the tribes of Israel. Around the stones, he dug a deep trench, then he placed the wood and bull on top. He had water poured on it three times. There was so much water that it ran everywhere on the altar and completely filled the trench!

1 KINGS

KEY POINTS

Elijah told the people of Israel to commit to God or Baal (1 Kings 18:21).

Elijah proved on Mount Carmel who the one true God really is (1 Kings 18:38-39).

So, after listening to hundreds of Baal's prophets run around raving all day, Elijah prayed a simple prayer to God. You can read 1 Kings 18:38–39 to see how God sent a fire that burned the wood and the bull and the stones and the water. Then the people recognized that God is the one true God! It must have been a very exciting moment to see God display His power like that.

The next thing God did was probably just as exciting to them. After three years of drought, He sent rain. That was another statement of power because the people thought Baal controlled the weather!

There was no doubt that day that God is the one true God. Thankfully, we can know that He is God without a miracle burning a trench full of water. We can learn from the story of Elijah. We can always honor God as the one and only true God.

PRAYER

The people of Israel had not been loyal to God, but they were reminded that He is the only one who deserves worship. We can be grateful to the Lord that we can learn from the example of the Israelites and avoid making the same mistakes. You can ask God to help you recognize if there are any things that take your attention away from Him. You can ask Him to help you always remember that He is the one true God.

2 KINGS

GOD'S UNSEEN ARMY

TEXT TRUTH

We do not need to be able to see what God is doing to trust that He is working in our lives.

EXAMINE THE TEXT

2 KINGS 6:16-19

Israel was in big trouble. The people had spent so many years disobeying God that they were facing the consequences through evil kings and internal division. Israel was not even one kingdom anymore! Because of their idolatry, there were problems ahead that were worse than they were already experiencing. Still, God was patient and sent prophets to prepare them and give them opportunities to repent. One person in particular was a prophet named Elisha.

Elisha is sometimes confused with the prophet he replaced, Elijah. Even though there were many similarities in their stories, they were very different. One of the biggest differences was their interaction with the kings of their time. Unlike Elijah, Elisha was often asked to counsel a king. He was willing to help, not because the king deserved it, but because he wanted to share God's message.

During a time of struggle against Syria, his help saved the king's life many times. The Syrian king was frustrated and thought that someone was telling secret plans to the king of Israel.

MEMORY VERSE

2 KINGS 6:16
Elisha said, "Don't be afraid, for those who are with us outnumber those who are with them."

149

2 KINGS

KEY POINTS

We can trust God to be with us, even though we cannot see Him (2 Kings 6:17).

When he discovered that Elisha was able to know his plans, he decided to capture him. The king of Syria knew that he would not be able to keep Elisha from knowing his secrets, but he thought he could keep him from telling the king of Israel.

When the Syrian king discovered Elisha's location, he sent a large army to surround the city. A servant, who was probably very nervous, asked Elisha what they should do. His response is in 2 Kings 6:16. Elisha was not afraid because he knew the great Syrian army was no match for the very special army protecting him. In verse 17 Elisha prayed for God to show the servant what Elisha already knew. Elisha knew there would be nothing to fear because of God's unseen army. When you keep reading 2 Kings 6:18–19, you will see that God caused the Syrian army to be blinded, and Elisha led them to Samaria. They learned their lesson and never returned to raid Israel again. What an amazing story of God's protection!

Elisha trusted God. He was not afraid, even though the king from Syria specifically targeted him. He knew God's power and authority. There are times in every person's life when there are choices between faith and fear. It is usually tempting to be afraid, but it seems like faith might have been a very easy choice for Elisha.

We can learn from Elisha's example to trust God. He shows us God's presence in our lives and how to rely on Him. Elisha knew that God was with him. We might not be able to see God or what He is doing in our lives, but we can trust that He is there. Any time situations in life cause fear, we can remember Elisha's example and be confident in God.

BATTLE GEAR

Soldiers in Old Testament times protected themselves with heavy armor such as breastplates, helmets, and shields.

PRAYER

Elisha knew that the threat against him was not enough to challenge God. He trusted in God's protection. He knew God was with him. You can ask the Lord to help you have the same confidence in His presence. You can ask Him to help you trust Him when you are afraid or need reassurance that He is in control.

2 CHRONICLES
THE BOOK OF THE LAW IS FOUND

TEXT TRUTH

Those who are truly committed to God will read the Bible and obey what they learn from it.

EXAMINE THE TEXT

2 CHRONICLES 34:14, 29-30

Can you imagine being a king? It would be quite a responsibility. Imagine becoming a king at the age of eight! That is what happened with one person who reigned for thirty-one years. There were many different kings who ruled over the Israelite people. You might remember that the kingdom of Israel had divided. One of the kings who lived in the southern kingdom, called Judah, was named Josiah. Josiah's father did not follow God, and some of his own people killed him. When Josiah's father died, Josiah was appointed as the new king even though he was only eight years old.

Josiah was loyal to God and tried to obey as well as he could. He tore down the altars and other structures that had been built to worship other gods. He also began a project to repair the temple. That project uncovered something very important just as the project was beginning. We can see in 2 Chronicles 34:14 that as the money was being gathered and handed over

MEMORY VERSE

2 CHRONICLES 34:14
When they brought out the silver that had been deposited in the LORD's temple, the priest Hilkiah found the book of the law of the LORD written by the hand of Moses.

to those responsible for the repairs, the priest found the book of the Law!

The Israelites were given the book of the Law through Moses. It was their guide. It was the Israelites' most important possession, and they had lost it. They lost it! That shows how far from God they had actually strayed. They were not even keeping up with the book of the Law. Finding it was both a terrible and wonderful moment for Josiah. Even though he was thrilled to have it back, he knew that it was more evidence of Israel's rebellion. He knew there would be consequences.

Second Chronicles 34:29–30 tells us that Josiah read it to everyone! He wanted everyone to know God's expectations. He renewed a commitment to God and commanded everyone to join him. This was not only an effort to turn things around as a nation, but it was also a true commitment to God.

In modern times, local shepherds found ancient manuscripts of Old Testament writings in the Qumran caves near the Dead Sea in Israel. The sacred writings had been stored in earthenware jars to keep them safe.

DEAD SEA SCROLLS

2 CHRONICLES

Josiah wanted to obey God and valued the book of the Law (2 Chronicles 34:30).

KEY POINTS

We can evaluate our obedience to God by how well we obey the Bible (2 Chronicles 34:21).

Josiah genuinely wanted to obey. There might have been people who did not share Josiah's excitement. It was probably difficult to adjust to following God's commands after all that time.

We can test our own attitudes toward God by asking ourselves how we might have responded or by comparing how we feel about the Bible. God wants us to treasure the Bible. It is a special message directly from Him. The Israelites did not appreciate the book of the Law, and they drifted away from what God wanted. If we spend time with God by reading the Bible, we will be more likely to avoid that same mistake. It is a privilege to have God's Word because we can know Him and know what He wants for our lives.

PRAYER

Josiah wanted to obey God, and he appreciated finding the book of the Law. He wanted to correct what was happening in Israel by encouraging everyone to follow God. You can talk to God about ways that you can obey Him and encourage others to obey Him. You might want to thank the Lord for the Bible and ask Him to help you apply what you learn when you read it.

PHILIPPIANS
GRUMBLING IS NOT LOVELY

TEXT TRUTH

We are able to avoid complaining when we focus on the right things.

EXAMINE THE TEXT

PHILIPPIANS 2:14; 4:8

It seems like Philippians 2:14 is one of the most difficult verses to obey. According to that verse, we should not complain or argue. That might seem simple, but we know it isn't. It is so easy to complain and argue that it is tempting to complain about having to obey that verse! There are many opportunities every single day to argue or complain. Sometimes it can almost be like a habit to make it known that we do not like things or insist on our own ways. Thankfully, when we focus on the right things, we are better able to obey God's instructions.

This verse is giving us good advice for how to get along with others, but it is also something much more important than that. It is telling us one of the ways that we can be like Jesus. The book of Philippians is very helpful in teaching us ways we can show our faith in Christ. It explains how Jesus humbled Himself for us and how His example can be our guide through life. We honor God when we obey His Word. This verse tells us a way to honor God every single day.

There are other benefits to applying this verse to our lives. We will be an example to others because they will see us reflecting Christ. It will also help us get along with people better.

MEMORY VERSE

PHILIPPIANS 2:14
Do everything without grumbling and arguing.

PHILIPPIANS

One of the most important things that will happen in your life is how you impact the people around you. Others will think more carefully about the way they live when they see you living for God.

Of course, it is all easier to think about than to actually do. So we can use Philippians 4:8 to prepare ourselves before the opportunity to argue or complain ever comes up. If you fill your mind with honorable, pure, lovely, excellent kinds of things, there will be no room for the things that make you feel like grumbling. These are purposeful thoughts that can prepare you for whatever happens each day.

When we only look at this one verse, we might think something is too difficult to do, but God does not give us commands that are impossible to follow. He gives us everything we need to obey Him. If you focus on lovely things, you are less likely to be tempted to complain. We have the ability to see things more clearly, and things are easier to accomplish.

KEY POINTS

If we focus on good things, we are less tempted to argue or complain (Philippians 4:8).

PRAYER

Although it might sometimes seem impossible to avoid complaining and arguing, it is possible. You can ask God to help you recognize times when you are tempted to argue or complain. You can thank Him for helping you see ways that you can obey Him every day. You can also ask God to give you patience with others and appreciation for them too.

ANCIENT JAIL

When Paul was in prison, he sang hymns to God to show his joy even in the midst of tough circumstances. The ruins of this prison in Philippi may be like the prison where Paul and Silas were held. God sent an earthquake to release them.

COLOSSIANS

JESUS IS GOD

TEXT TRUTH

Living for Jesus is more than simply following a good example; it is living for God.

MEMORY VERSE

COLOSSIANS 2:9
The entire fullness of God's nature dwells bodily in Christ.

EXAMINE THE TEXT

COLOSSIANS 2:6-9; 1:19; 3:12-17

Paul wrote Colossians to a group of people who had been facing some problems. Their understanding of salvation was being corrupted by some false teachings. The biggest problem was that people claimed that Jesus was not God. Because they did not think He was God, they did not believe that Jesus' sacrifice on the cross was enough to pay for sin. This confusion led to doubts about how to live and what religious practices to follow. Paul was very helpful to guide the believers back to a clear understanding. He reminded them of their faith and what it should look like in everyday life. Mostly he reminded them of the one true God.

When you read Colossians 2:6–9, you will see that Paul encouraged the people at the Colossian church to live for Jesus. He reminded them of their salvation and what they already knew about the Lord. This was to help them invalidate all the false teachings that were being introduced. Paul wanted to make it clear that those lies were not from God.

In verse 9, Paul used the word *deity* (NIV). It is pronounced, "dee-ih-tee." Basically it means God. This verse says that Jesus has the fullness of deity. If you compare it to Colossians 1:19, you will see that both verses identify Jesus as having the fullness of God.

That means Jesus is completely and totally God! It also means that there is no need for anything else to provide salvation. He is enough. Jesus' death on the cross was the perfect sacrifice. Nothing else could accomplish what He did, and nothing else is required.

JESUS IS THE CORNERSTONE

The Bible describes Jesus as the cornerstone. A cornerstone is the corner foundation piece that supports the foundation and direction of the building. Jesus is the foundation of our faith. Our faith depends on the life, death, and resurrection of Jesus.

COLOSSIANS

KEY POINTS

Jesus is God (Colossians 2:9).

Jesus' sacrifice on the cross was all that was needed to pay for sin (Colossians 2:14).

We have the Bible to tell us how to live for Jesus (Colossians 3:16).

There are no other ideas or thoughts or philosophies or teachings that can undo what the Bible tells us about Jesus. He is God. People will try to suggest that the Bible is not true or that there are other books just as holy as the Bible, but we do not have to be fooled. Those are the same types of arguments people made to the Colossian church, and we know that Paul's instructions for them are just as helpful for us.

We can remember who Jesus is and live for Him. Colossians 3:12–17 shows us some ways we can live for Jesus. We can be thankful, patient, forgiving, and so much more. These verses tell us many ways to help us recognize what being a Christian looks like. We do not have to be distracted by those who try to make other claims about Jesus or how His followers should behave. We have the Bible to give us the truth.

PRAYER

Paul wrote the book of Colossians to help people who were confused about Jesus, about how He saves sinners, and about how their lives should reflect salvation. We can be thankful that we have the Bible to help us understand who Jesus is and how to live for Him. You can thank Him for letting us know that He is all that is necessary for salvation. You can ask God to show you how to serve Him and work heartily for Him.

PHILEMON
A SERVANT FOR GOD

TEXT TRUTH

A life lived for God will impact others, so we should be willing to repent and forgive.

EXAMINE THE TEXT

PHILEMON

Some things you will read in the Bible are very helpful and easy to understand. Other things will be confusing. The book of Philemon tells an interesting and wonderful story, but the people involved were in a very confusing situation. Paul was in prison in Rome, and a dear friend was helping care for him. This friend's name was Onesimus. It is pronounced "Oh-nee-see-muss." Paul loved Onesimus. He considered him to be a great help and a true friend. Unfortunately, before Onesimus became a follower of Jesus, he had made some poor choices.

Not only did Onesimus run away from a man named Philemon, but he may have also stolen money from Philemon. Onesimus had been Philemon's servant. When he ran away, he went to Rome where no one would notice him. He met Paul, and Paul introduced him to Jesus. Once Onesimus had faith in Christ, he made different choices. His life was not the same. So he decided to return to Philemon and ask for forgiveness.

MEMORY VERSE

PHILEMON 1:6
I pray that your participation in the faith may become effective through knowing every good thing that is in us for the glory of Christ.

PHILEMON

KEY POINTS

It is more important to live for God than it is to live for ourselves (Philemon 1:6).

We need to be willing to repent and forgive (Philemon 1:10, 17).

Others will see how we live for God (Philemon 1:5).

Philemon was not legally obligated to forgive him, but Paul knew there was a greater obligation in his life. You see, Philemon had met Paul years earlier. He was also a Christian. Paul appealed to him to forgive Onesimus and accept him back as a fellow believer.

This was an amazing situation. Onesimus was so devoted to God that he was willing to return to a life of servanthood to live as pure a life as possible. This was a true dedication to repentance. There was no guarantee that Philemon would appreciate his apology. So Onesimus had only one thing to gain by returning—a clear conscience before God. That is an excellent example of devotion. We can see in Philemon 1:6 that Paul was encouraging Philemon to have that same level of devotion. This situation would be widely known. Paul wanted Philemon to recognize the influence his decision would have and how it would reflect his faith in God.

You might be wondering why Paul did not openly insist that Philemon free Onesimus. The Bible does not tell us, but even without all the answers to this complicated situation, we can see that it is an example of repentance, Christian support, obedience to God, and so much more. You can remember the book of Philemon when you need courage to follow through with something you know God wants you to do. It can help you stay focused on God and how to live for Him, know how your life will influence others, and be willing to repent as well as forgive.

HIDDEN MONEY

Onesimus was a slave who stole money from his owners. During the time of the New Testament, many people in Israel hid their money and valuables in hoards like this one, so it wouldn't be taken. The coins inside let us know when the hoards were hidden. This one is from the disciples' time and was found outside of Jericho.

PRAYER

You can thank the Lord for teaching us through the Bible and for showing us that even when situations are not perfect, people can still serve Him. You can ask God to help you recognize ways you can be more forgiving, have the right attitude toward others, and see people the way He wants you to see them. You can also ask God to help you when you need to ask others for forgiveness.

OBADIAH
YOU HAVE BEEN WARNED

TEXT TRUTH

We should focus on living for God and trust His ability to judge the sins of others.

MEMORY VERSE

OBADIAH 1:15
The day of the LORD is near, against all the nations. As you have done, it will be done to you; what you deserve will return on your own head.

EXAMINE THE TEXT

OBADIAH 1:15

As important as it is to know the mercy of God, we cannot completely appreciate it until we understand the judgment of God. The book of Obadiah shows us that God's patience will not allow sin to continue forever. He will ultimately hold people accountable. God is patient to allow people the opportunity to repent. The nation of Edom exhausted their opportunities.

If you have read the book of Genesis, you might remember twin brothers named Jacob and Esau. They spent many years struggling against one another. Then their descendants became two entire nations that struggled against one another. Edom was the nation that began through Esau. They were enemies of Israel, the nation that began through Jacob. The Edomites mistreated Israel, which was a symbolic rejection of God. After all, these were His chosen people.

The Edomites lived in the clefts of rock in southern Judah. They believed their narrow canyons and rock fortresses would protect them from invasion. The Edomites and Israelites fought each other for centuries. But Obadiah claimed that God would punish Edom. In battle with the Edomites, the armies of Judah struck down 10,000 Edomites and threw 10,000 more off a cliff like these.

The book of Obadiah tells us of Edom's judgment. It is an unsettling book, but it is also comforting. God was being consistent. He gave Edom time to repent and preserved Israel. Those are things we can see happening over and over throughout the Old Testament. It is something we can always expect.

Obadiah 1:15 is a warning that whatever is done will be judged. That warning is for more than Edom. It is to all nations over time. Everyone should have the same expectation of judgment. That is what sin brings. It always brings judgment.

Thankfully, we know there is hope. We can be restored through faith in Jesus. Our judgment can be satisfied by His sacrifice. What a relief! For those who trust in Christ, there is no fear of eternal judgment. We can focus on living for Him and making the most of our time on earth.

There is also another kind of relief that comes with knowing God will judge sin. We can be free of any feelings of revenge. It is terrible when people are mean or hurtful. It can cause us to feel sad or afraid or angry.

OBADIAH

God judges sin (Obadiah 1:15).

Those who have faith in Christ have no eternal judgment to fear (Romans 5:1).

God's judgment is perfect (Obadiah 1:15).

Sometimes we might want to mistreat people because they mistreated us. That is not the way God wants us to respond. He wants us to let Him judge sin.

We have an example to follow any time we encounter a person who is being difficult. We are supposed to treat them the way the Israelites were told to treat the Edomites. We should not retaliate when someone mistreats us. God will handle all offenses against us. We can trust Him to deal with things the way He determines is best. God's judgment is always perfect.

Thinking about God's judgment can make us uncomfortable because we all sin. The book of Obadiah shows us that God does exactly what He says He will do. Yes, we all sin, but we do not all have to face judgment. God is patient and merciful and loving. He will not tolerate sin, but He forgives those who repent and trust in Jesus.

PRAYER

The book of Obadiah shows us the terrible consequences of sin. We can rejoice that God provided a way for our judgment to be met through Jesus. You can talk to God about His judgment of sin and ask Him to help you understand salvation and how it affects His judgment of sin. You can also thank Him for being trustworthy with His judgment and generous with His mercy.

EZEKIEL
TURN BACK, TURN BACK

TEXT TRUTH

God's threat of judgment is serious, so we can be grateful for His willingness to forgive.

EXAMINE THE TEXT

EZEKIEL 5:1-5

When God decides to take action, He means business. It is easy for us to forget that sin is a serious problem with serious consequences. We can sometimes confuse God's patience with His approval, but God never approves of sin. He does not overlook it or forget. He does not punish immediately because He allows time for people to repent. When people do not repent, they are accepting the consequences. The book of Ezekiel describes a situation that was very serious for Jerusalem. The people of Israel needed to repent, but they did not take God's warnings seriously.

The prophet Ezekiel was given instructions to describe what was on the way for Jerusalem.

Ezekiel 5:1–5 tells about what must have been one of the most unusual haircuts of all time! Not only was Ezekiel told to use a sword to cut his beard and hair, but he was also required to weigh what he cut off and divide it into thirds. Ezekiel 5:12 tells

MEMORY VERSE

EZEKIEL 33:11

Tell them, "As I live–this is the declaration of the LORD God –I take no pleasure in the death of the wicked, but rather that the wicked person should turn from his way and live. Repent, repent of your evil ways! Why will you die, house of Israel?"

EZEKIEL

Jerusalem became an example to everyone (Ezekiel 5:5).

God warns of the consequences of sin (Ezekiel 5:8-9).

God is willing to forgive (Ezekiel 18:21).

us what it all meant. Ezekiel was told to burn some of his hair, strike some with a sword, and scatter some. That symbolized that a third of the people would be consumed with famine and disease, a third would be killed by the sword, and a third would die in exile. A very small number would be saved out of Jerusalem, so it was almost complete destruction!

The people were given time to repent, but they did not take it seriously. In the past, many things threatened to destroy Jerusalem without success, so they were not worried. They felt confident they could continue on as they had been. They were wrong. They were not listening to God.

The same thing happens today. Many people are not paying attention to the Bible. They are not thinking about the consequences of their sin. That is a mistake.

God always punishes sin. Every sin will be punished, and everyone is a sinner. That means we are all accountable. The only hope we have is in Jesus. His sacrifice on the cross

paid the penalty for sin. God offers grace through faith in Jesus, and that saving faith always includes repentance. We can see in Ezekiel 33:11 that God wants repentance. That is why the people of Jerusalem were in such trouble. They did not take the opportunity given to them by God. He allowed time for them to repent, but they carried on in their rebellion instead.

God wants you to live for Him, and He does not give empty warnings. He will punish sin. Thankfully, He will also forgive. When you think of your attitude toward God, you might want to ask yourself if you have faith that leads to repentance. It can help you recognize things in your life that require a prayer of repentance. It is too late for the people to whom Ezekiel spoke, but you still have the opportunity to turn from sin and turn to God.

PRAYER

God gave us examples like this one from the book of Ezekiel to help us understand His judgment and willingness to forgive. We can thank Him for these examples and all the other ways we are able to know Him. You can ask God to help you recognize sin in your life and to help you turn from your sin to Him. You can thank God for being willing to forgive sin, and if you trust Him, ask Him to forgive you.

God told Ezekiel to cut his beard with a sword. This illustration shows a typical sword that would have been used in Ezekiel's time.

THE HAIRCUT

DANIEL
BOW ONLY TO GOD

EXAMINE THE TEXT

DANIEL 3:16-18

If you are familiar with today's Bible story, you will recognize it as an exciting example of devotion to God.

MEMORY VERSE

DANIEL 3:18

Even if he does not rescue us, we want you as king to know that we will not serve your gods or worship the gold statue you set up.

The story begins with the king of the Babylonian Empire. His name was Nebuchadnezzar. He was very proud of himself and had a huge image of his likeness built out of gold. It was common at that time for a national leader to require that his people follow a particular religion. They knew that such a strong connection always helped unite an entire nation. That appears to be what Nebuchadnezzar was attempting to do.

Along with the ordinary citizens, he gathered together all the government officials and military leaders. The king insisted that everyone bow down to his golden image in worship. When specific music played, everyone was expected to bow. King Nebuchadnezzar had a punishment ready for anyone who refused to bow down and worship his image. He told them they would be thrown into a fiery furnace.

Three young men named Shadrach, Meshach, and Abednego refused to bow. Their rebellion was reported to the king, and he called for them to be brought before him. He was angry, and he told them his expectations again. He warned that if they did not bow down and worship his image when they heard the music that they would be thrown into the fiery furnace.

King Nebuchadnezzar thought that he was the one with all the power to control the situation. He asked who would save them from his punishment, but he became very angry when he heard their response. You can see it in Daniel 3:16–18. Shadrach, Meshach, and Abednego told Nebuchadnezzar that the one true God had the power to save them and could rescue them. They knew God would reveal Himself if that was His choice.

There was one important point that they made clear to everyone. Whether God saved them or not, they wanted it known that they would not bow down and worship King Nebuchadnezzar's golden image or anything else. That was not what the king wanted to hear!

Nebuchadnezzar began his rise to power during a time of conflict between Babylon and Egypt. After Nebuchadnezzar secured his territory, he called young men to train to serve in his palace. Check out this map of ancient Babylon. Nebuchadnezzar's courts were likely just inside the main gate.

He demanded that the furnace be heated seven times hotter than usual. His men tied up Shadrach, Meshach, and Abednego and threw them into the furnace. It was so hot that the heat killed the men who threw them in!

DANIEL

Shadrach, Meshach, and Abednego would only worship God (Daniel 3:18).

KEY POINTS

They were loyal to God even though they did not know if He would save them (Daniel 3:17-18).

God is the only one worthy of worship (Daniel 3:28-29).

When Shadrach, Meshach, and Abednego fell into the furnace, something miraculous happened. Instead of three men bound in the fire, there were four men walking around in it unharmed. A heavenly being was with Shadrach, Meshach, and Abednego in the furnace. When they were taken out, they had no burns, not even singed hair or the smell of smoke. God had protected the men!

There was probably a lot of pressure on those young men. They were standing before a king. The entire kingdom had bowed down already. But they stood for God anyway. This story is a terrific example of how we can trust God. Hopefully you will not face a threat as serious as a fiery furnace, but you can remember Shadrach, Meshach, and Abednego anytime you need courage to stand firm in your faith.

PRAYER

There is only one God, and He is the only one worthy of worship. You can thank God for the example of Shadrach, Meshach, and Abednego, and ask Him to help you have courage the way they did. Since idolatry will probably look different today than it did with King Nebuchadnezzar, you might want to ask God to help you recognize it in your life. You can also ask Him to help you worship only Him and trust in His protection.

JEREMIAH
SUCCEED WITH GOD

TEXT TRUTH

Even when we do not see positive results, we should continue to obey God.

EXAMINE THE TEXT

JEREMIAH 1:7

People usually measure success by the results of our effort. Most of the time we can look at the outcome to see whether or not we met a goal. Even though that might work in many circumstances, it is not the way God measures success. Truthfully, sometimes being a success for God looks like complete failure to everyone else.

A prophet named Jeremiah was a dedicated messenger of God who was treated terribly by those he was sent to warn. The people of Israel were not impressed with Jeremiah, but we can look at his life and see that he was truly successful in his faithfulness to God.

Jeremiah spread God's warnings for Judah, but the people did not listen. Instead, they enjoyed the messages of the false prophets who made them think everything would be great. They rejected Jeremiah's message from God because it promised punishment instead of prosperity. You might think the rejection of the people would be enough to discourage Jeremiah, but he continued to share God's message for more than forty years.

MEMORY VERSE

JEREMIAH 1:7
The LORD said to me: Do not say, "I am only a youth," for you will go to everyone I send you to and speak whatever I tell you.

JEREMIAH

Jeremiah continued to obey God no matter what happened (Jeremiah 26:14-15).

KEY POINTS

We should obey God, even if others oppose us (Jeremiah 1:8).

Jeremiah is known as the weeping prophet for the anguish he had over the people's rebellion and the coming judgment. He is also known for the mistreatment he endured. In one incident, some officials accused Jeremiah of wanting harm to come to the people. Instead of recognizing that it was a message from God, they blamed Jeremiah for causing bad things to happen.

Jeremiah warned that Babylon would take over the city. He suggested that people go out and submit before they were killed. Some of the officials considered him a traitor for making a claim that their enemy would defeat them. They told the king that Jeremiah was affecting the people's outlook, which was dangerous. The king did not protect Jeremiah and allowed the officials to take him away. They threw him into a cistern, which is basically a deep pit where water is collected. This particular cistern did not have water, but Jeremiah sank into the mud at the bottom. He was saved from the pit, but it did not change the rebellion of the people. They continued to ignore his messages from God, and Babylon eventually overthrew Judah.

Jeremiah was rejected, mistreated, ignored, and thrown into a pit. His words were never taken seriously, and he never convinced the Israelites to repent and follow God's instructions. Even with all that, Jeremiah is an example of enormous success. He continued to obey God, no matter how people treated him. He did not look to the results among the people as his measure of success. He knew God had a different standard for him.

When Jeremiah was young, he was given the message of Jeremiah 1:7, and it can be an encouragement to you like it was to him. He was told not to be discouraged by his youth but to go speak for God. You can obey God right now, and remember Jeremiah's determined obedience anytime you are not getting the results you expect to get in your life. Obeying God is always successful.

DEEP PIT

Cisterns in the ancient world were bottle- or pear-shaped wells deep in the ground in which people kept water—often LOTS of water. Sometimes these deep, dark holes were used for temporary prisons. They were even used as dumping places for dead bodies.

LAMENTATIONS

THE SORROW OF SIN

TEXT TRUTH

Sin will always cause sorrow, so we need to look to God for comfort and hope.

EXAMINE THE TEXT

LAMENTATIONS 3:26

A *dirge* is a funeral song. It expresses mourning over a loss. The book of Lamentations is a dirge for the loss of Jerusalem. You might remember that the prophet Jeremiah warned of the coming judgment for forty years.

MEMORY VERSE

LAMENTATIONS 3:26
It is good to wait quietly for salvation from the LORD.

He was treated poorly and rejected because the people did not want to hear what he had to say. He continued to obey God while the rest of the Israelites refused to repent. Over the years God had used different consequences to direct the people back to Him, but they kept repeating their pattern of sin until He eventually took back the land He had given them. Although Jeremiah was not treated well, he loved the people and was very sad over their rebellion. He mourned for them.

His anguish is described in Lamentations in a very interesting way. The first four chapters create acrostic patterns. That means that the first letter of each verse or section of verses corresponds with a letter of the Hebrew alphabet. It might have been written that way to help people remember it. We should definitely remember it because it helps us understand the consequences of sin and the importance of living for God. We can also look to the book of Lamentations to help us in times of sorrow. Sin always causes sorrow.

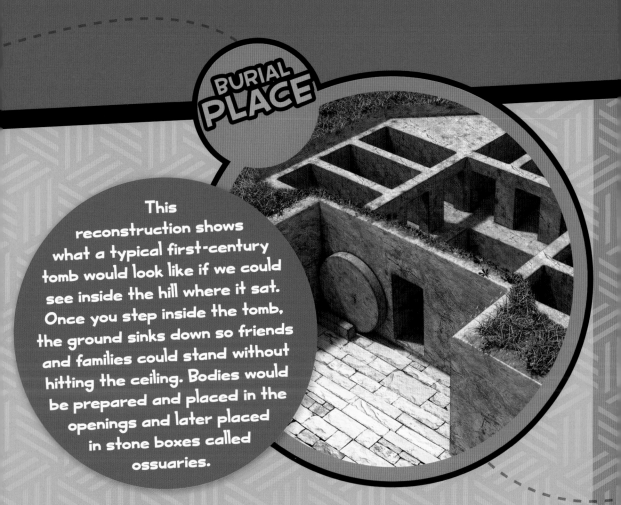

This reconstruction shows what a typical first-century tomb would look like if we could see inside the hill where it sat. Once you step inside the tomb, the ground sinks down so friends and families could stand without hitting the ceiling. Bodies would be prepared and placed in the openings and later placed in stone boxes called ossuaries.

Lamentations can help us find hope in our sadness.

You have probably had moments in your life when you were sad. Maybe it was because of something simple like losing a favorite toy, or it might have been something more serious like losing a person you love. Those moments can make us feel devastated. We can avoid the sorrow caused by our own sin by repenting, but we cannot always influence what someone else does. That can be difficult, because everyone's sin can cause consequences for others.

The situation in Lamentations was a consequence of sin. The people were not willing to repent, and they paid dearly. We might not always think of sorrow as a consequence of sin, but it is easy to see that it is when we think of how it affected Jeremiah. It was not his sin, yet he suffered.

Lamentations 3:16–18 is a vivid description of sorrow, which is a hopeless feeling that can be overwhelming.

LAMENTATIONS

KEY POINTS

Sin always causes sorrow (Lamentations 1:16).

God offers comfort and hope (Lamentations 3:24).

When Jeremiah wrote this, he felt the full agony of his emotions, but he was always still aware of God's presence and sovereignty. He knew that there was more beyond his grief.

Lamentations 3:22–26 reminds us that God does not leave us in sorrow. His plan for us is full of love and mercy and hope. We can always turn to God in times of sorrow. He offers a comfort that cannot be found anywhere else. We can trust Him to guide us to better things beyond our sadness.

PRAYER

Jeremiah's grief was obvious in the book of Lamentations. Even though he felt terrible sorrow, he always trusted God. God has allowed us to know how Jeremiah handled sorrow, and He will help us follow the same example when we experience sadness. You can ask God to guide you through the overwhelming feelings when something devastating happens. Trust Him for the hope that only He can give.

HEBREWS
SEE GOD IN SCRIPTURE

EXAMINE THE TEXT

HEBREWS 11:1; 9:11-12

You might remember from the book of James that we should make sure we are living out our faith. We can think something, but it is not meaningful if we do not live differently. Our actions expose what we really believe. The book of Hebrews includes many examples of those who lived in a way that revealed great faith. Many people call them heroes of faith because they are such good examples of what it looks like to trust God. Genuine faith will be expressed. That means the result of faith will be visible, but the object of faith is not. No one can see God, but they can see what you believe by seeing how you live.

MEMORY VERSE

HEBREWS 11:1

Faith is the reality of what is hoped for, the proof of what is not seen.

Hebrews 11:1 defines faith. If you are fully convinced of something that you cannot see, you have faith. All of us are challenged to trust in a God who is not visible to us. So to know God we must gather all the knowledge and wisdom we can gain from the Bible. It is God's message to us that we can hold and see and use to learn about Him.

HEBREWS

Faith is trusting the God we cannot see (Hebrews 11:1).

KEY POINTS

We can know God through the Bible (Hebrews 11:3).

Jesus' sacrifice provided personal access to God (Hebrews 9:12).

The book of Hebrews is full of important information about God. One very important thing we should know is how Jesus completed what the sacrifices of the Old Covenant could not. You probably remember that the priests were required to offer sacrifices on behalf of the people. They had many different restrictions and things to consider. It was a complicated process that had to be done regularly.

Sins kept happening, so sacrifices kept having to be made. The priests were burdened to handle the sacrifices because it was a holy process. The high priest was the only one allowed into the most holy place, which was deeper inside the tent and behind a second curtain. These sacrifices had to be carried out in very precise ways, and they had to be repeated over and over again . . . until Jesus made the perfect sacrifice that made the daily sacrifices no longer necessary. You can read about that in Hebrews 9:11–12.

Jesus' sacrifice was only necessary one time to provide eternal life.

Because of Him, we can be forgiven of sin. We no longer need to go through a priest. We can pray directly to God. We can be with Him in heaven, and we do not need to see Him to know Him. When you read the Bible, you will discover who God is. You will not see Him with your eyes, but you can see Him through His Word. The Bible will teach you everything you need to know to have faith in God.

Only the high priest could enter the most holy place, which contained the ark of the covenant. This is where God's presence was. The high priest could only enter here once a year, on the day of atonement.

PRAYER

The things we can learn from the book of Hebrews and all the other books of the Bible will help us know God. If we know God through the Bible, it doesn't matter if we can see Him with our eyes. You can thank God for giving you a way to know Him. You can ask for help to know Him through what you learn in the Bible and ask Him to give you faith to trust Him for salvation.

ESTHER
FOR THIS VERY PURPOSE

TEXT TRUTH

God uses the circumstances and decisions of ordinary people to accomplish His plan.

EXAMINE THE TEXT

ESTHER 7:3-4

God is not named in the book of Esther. Instead, the story shows how His plans are fulfilled through the lives of ordinary people. It all began when the Persian king Ahasuerus demanded that his wife present herself during a large feast so he could show off her beauty. She refused, which insulted the king. He not only had her banished from the kingdom, but he also made a law that all women had to give honor to their husbands.

He chose a young woman named Esther to become the new queen. She was lovely, and the king was very impressed with her, but he did not know that she was Jewish. This was complicated because one of the king's highest-ranking officials, Haman, tricked him into implementing a plan to get rid of all the Jews in the empire. Haman disguised it as a plan to protect Persia, but it was motivated by his hatred for the Jewish people.

The king trusted Haman and enacted his plan. He sealed an edict that would annihilate the Jews.

MEMORY VERSE

ESTHER 7:3

Queen Esther answered, "If I have found favor in your eyes, Your Majesty, and if the king is pleased, spare my life; this is my request. And spare my people; this is my desire."

Although he did not know it at the time, the king's edict would have included his own queen. When Esther's cousin Mordecai learned of the plan to kill all the Jewish people, he sent a message to her. He insisted that she beg the king not to comply with the edict. It was a dangerous request because no one was allowed to enter the king's presence without being invited. If a person did appear before the king uninvited, the penalty was death, unless the king saved them by extending his golden scepter.

Esther was afraid to approach the king and resisted at first. Mordecai pointed out that even she would become subject to this evil plan. Then Mordecai told Esther the most memorable thing in the entire book of Esther. He commented that maybe God had ordered the events that made her the queen for this very purpose!

This scepter, made out of onyx, is from about 600 B.C.

The scepter was a symbol of the king's power. It was held out to visitors who were accepted before the throne. Scepters looked different in each kingdom but most were ornate with gold and precious stones. Esther waited for the king to extend his golden scepter to give his approval of her visit. Appearing before the king uninvited could have cost Esther her life!

ESTHER

KEY POINTS

God displays His sovereignty through ordinary people (Esther 4:14).

God gives us purpose (Esther 4:14).

We can have courage to fulfill our purpose for God (Esther 8:3).

When Esther thought about Mordecai's words, she agreed to approach the king, even though it was dangerous. Because there was a law forbidding anyone to enter his presence plus the law that women must honor their husbands, Esther did not know what to expect. Thankfully, when she approached the king, he welcomed her. She was safe to be in his presence, but she was still unsure how to make the request to save her people. The king still did not know that Esther was Jewish. We can see in Esther 7:3–4 that she finally got the courage to ask the king to save her people from annihilation. The king agreed, and the Jewish people were saved.

This is what it looks like when God uses ordinary events to work together to accomplish His plan. He does not have to be mentioned by name to be present in the circumstances. You might not always notice what God is doing in your life, but you can be confident that He is present and working things out for His purposes. You can trust God.

PRAYER

Esther was just an ordinary person who had an opportunity to do something important. Her purpose was from God. She can be an example to us to persevere in difficult circumstances. You can thank God for being in control as you navigate through life. You can ask Him to help you make good decisions and to give you courage and willingness to always follow through with what is right.

EZRA

BE STRONG AND DO IT

TEXT TRUTH

Returning to previous sins can create difficult problems; we should be strong and turn to God.

EXAMINE THE TEXT

EZRA 10:4

There is no doubt that the people of Israel needed many reminders to devote themselves to God. You might think that the destruction of Jerusalem would have been enough of a reminder, but it was not. In case you do not remember, the Israelites had been taken captive by the Babylonians. After spending seventy years in exile, they were allowed to return to Jerusalem. They had to rebuild the entire city, but they put off the construction of the temple. The prophets Zechariah and Haggai encouraged the people to focus on the Lord. This resulted in some changes that inspired the completion of the temple. It was all moving in a better direction, but there were still problems.

MEMORY VERSE

EZRA 10:4

Get up, for this matter is your responsibility, and we support you. Be strong and take action!

Time passed while they carried on with life. They began to commit many of their previous sins and were soon living as though they had never experienced God's earlier punishment. Ezra, an expert teacher, went to Jerusalem to teach God's law. He was surprised by what he saw. He recognized the people creating the same problems that had led to God's judgment.

EZRA

Be careful not to turn back to previous sins (Ezra 9:14).

Be willing to correct any problems sin causes (Ezra 10:4).

Always turn to God to overcome sin (Ezra 10:1).

He worried that the punishment for this offense would not be something they could overcome again. After all, this was a terrible insult to God.

Ezra was especially bothered that the men had married foreign wives. This was a huge issue not because the women were from somewhere else, but because they had corrupted God's people to accept their foreign gods as objects of worship. Ezra was so upset over this that he tore his clothes and ripped out his hair. He prayed on behalf of the people. His prayer was a confession of guilt that inspired the people to join him. They made a plan to change course and asked Ezra to lead them out of their situation. You can read what they told him in Ezra 10:4.

The people knew that it would be difficult to correct the many problems they had caused. They wanted Ezra to know that they were going to support him. Ezra had quite a task to help redirect what was happening among the Jewish people.

You might not have a problem with foreign wives and their foreign gods, but you might have certain sins that you return to. We all struggle with remembering what God has done for us. We each have different temptations and favorite sins that keep us distracted from God, but He does not allow excuses. Even though it is difficult to avoid our sins, we are still responsible to avoid them. Sometimes we might even have to clean up the mess that we cause by our choices. We might have to correct problems and apologize to others. It is important that we are willing to do whatever God requires. He will help us. No matter how many times we are tempted, no matter how many times we fail, the only way to overcome sin is to turn to God.

THE SCRIBE

The cast of an exercise tablet on which a student copied text

PRAYER

Ezra was able to see right away that there were problems among the Jewish people. They were not paying attention to their own decline, but when he pointed things out, they recognized their mistakes. You can thank God for the example of the Israelites that reveals to us the danger of returning to old patterns of sin. You can ask Him to help you do what is necessary to turn away from sin.

Scribes were educated and trained to record events and important decisions. While in exile, scribes like Ezra were priests and experts in God's Word—copying, preserving, and teaching the Scriptures. Writing was performed using a reed pen, sharpened with a knife, and scribes underwent formal training for the job. They had vast knowledge of the Scriptures, and were known as men of great wisdom and intelligence.

NEHEMIAH
REBUILDING A CITY

TEXT TRUTH

When we trust God, we can accomplish impossible things.

EXAMINE THE TEXT

NEHEMIAH 9:6

Sometimes one person can make a big difference. Nehemiah was certainly able to make a difference in Jerusalem. Of course, he did not do everything alone, but he influenced others to work together and turn to God. It changed everything.

The Israelites had been captured by the Babylonians and kept in exile for seventy years. After they were allowed to return to Jerusalem, they struggled to get everything repaired. Even though the temple had been restored years earlier, the city was still in disorder. The walls had not

MEMORY VERSE

NEHEMIAH 9:6

You, LORD, are the only God. You created the heavens, the highest heavens with all their stars, the earth and all that is on it, the seas and all that is in them. You give life to all of them, and all the stars of heaven worship you.

been repaired, so the people were not protected. Something had to change.

During the captivity in Babylon, Nehemiah served the king as a cupbearer. (This was a special job that required him to protect the king from being poisoned. Kings were often poisoned, so the cupbearer would guard the king's cup and taste the king's drinks.) Nehemiah was near the king because of his role as the cupbearer. The king noticed that Nehemiah was sad and asked why. Nehemiah explained that he had heard of problems in Jerusalem. He requested permission to go there to help, and the king allowed it.

When Nehemiah arrived, he was shocked to find things worse than he had expected. He made inspections, prayed, and gave instructions. The time had come for the people to dedicate themselves to rebuilding the walls. The people began working and immediately faced opposition. They had experienced similar problems before, but this time they would not be discouraged. Instead, they stood ready to defend themselves, and it frightened their enemies away. It did cause them to change the plan a bit.

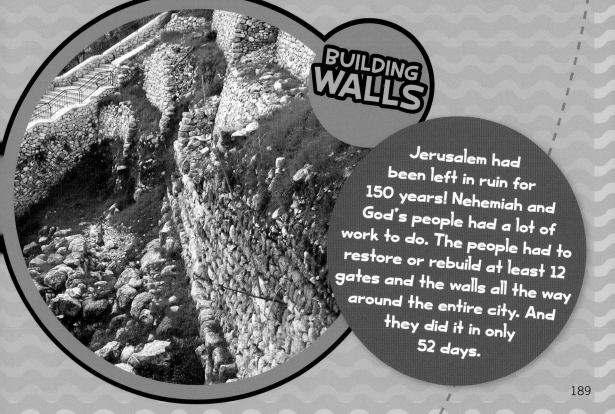

BUILDING WALLS

Jerusalem had been left in ruin for 150 years! Nehemiah and God's people had a lot of work to do. The people had to restore or rebuild at least 12 gates and the walls all the way around the entire city. And they did it in only 52 days.

NEHEMIAH

Nehemiah was able to do impossible things because he trusted God (Nehemiah 2:20).

KEY POINTS

God is worthy of worship (Nehemiah 9:6).

Half the people working stood guard, and the other half kept their swords with them as they built the walls. Nehemiah also helped those in need, and he dealt with people trying to trick him and intimidate him. It was quite a job, but they accomplished everything they set out to do in only fifty-two days! It would not have been possible to gather the supplies, get everyone's support, and protect themselves from their enemies without God's help. Nehemiah knew that and was always depending on the Lord for help.

Once the wall was built, Ezra invited everyone to assemble as he read the book of the Law. The people were moved by what they heard and worshiped God. They were challenged to think about their sin. They confessed and acknowledged God. You can read Nehemiah 9:6 to see how the Israelites were reminded by Nehemiah that God was still worthy of worship. They remembered His mercy and all that He had done for them.

When we get overwhelmed or let sin go on too long, it can feel as though we have no hope of getting back on track. Trusting God will always redirect our paths. Nehemiah trusted God and was able to guide the people to accomplish things they could not have done on their own. We can remember their example to trust God and stay focused on Him in everything we do.

PRAYER

The Jewish people struggled to stay focused on God. We can learn from their struggle to avoid their mistakes and turn to Him when we make similar ones. You can ask God to help you always keep Him as the main focus of your life and to help you turn to Him quickly if you fail to do that. You can also thank God for His patience and mercy and willingness to help you when you need Him.

HABAKKUK

TRUST GOD ANYWAY

TEXT TRUTH

God will not always do things in a way that we can understand, but He deserves our trust anyway.

EXAMINE THE TEXT

HABAKKUK 1:5

Sometimes we might feel frustrated that God is not handling a problem the way we think He should. That is what was happening with the prophet Habakkuk. The book of Habakkuk does not tell us of any message he was delivering to God's people. Instead, it tells us of one prophet's own struggles with what he was seeing in the world.

Habakkuk was bothered that righteous people seemed to suffer while evil people seemed to get away with everything. He wondered why God was not acting. He wanted people punished or rewarded according to his assessment of what they deserved.

He asked God why nothing was being done. Habakkuk 1:5 shows God's response. God basically told Habakkuk that he would not believe the plan even if God told it to him.

That is usually the way things happen with God. He does things that we would not expect or imagine or understand. The circumstances were not clear to Habakkuk. Nothing was in place for Habakkuk to see what was coming.

MEMORY VERSE

HABAKKUK 1:5
"Look at the nations and observe—be utterly astounded! For I am doing something in your days that you will not believe when you hear about it."

HABAKKUK

We will
not always
understand
God's plan
(Habakkuk 1:5).

We can
trust God even
when we do not know
everything He is doing
(Habakkuk 2:3-4).

God deserves
our trust no
matter what
(Habakkuk 3:18).

He had no concept of God's plan, so he asked for more information. He was not satisfied that things were going to be taken care of. He wanted justice.

God shared some details with Habakkuk, but that was not enough. Habakkuk had more questions of why God was planning to do things a certain way. Through it all God helped Habakkuk recognize His righteousness. He removed the need to accomplish things Habakkuk's way by reminding him that those who live by faith will be preserved God's way. In the end, Habakkuk recognized that God had His own purposes in how He did things. Habakkuk did not need to understand all of God's ways in order to trust Him.

There will be times in your life when you do not understand what God is doing or why He is not handling a problem the way you think He should. It will be helpful to remember Habakkuk's example during those times. We do not need to approve of God's methods or even understand them. We only need to know that

God is righteous. God deserves to be worshiped whether we understand what He is doing or not. He is God. There is purpose in everything He does. He does not make mistakes and does not get off course.

Sometimes we might be able to make sense of something that we do not like. Other times we might never be able to recognize any purpose for it at all. That is all right, because God does. He is in control and will handle it better than we could ever imagine. We will not always see everything God is doing, but we can live by faith and trust Him anyway.

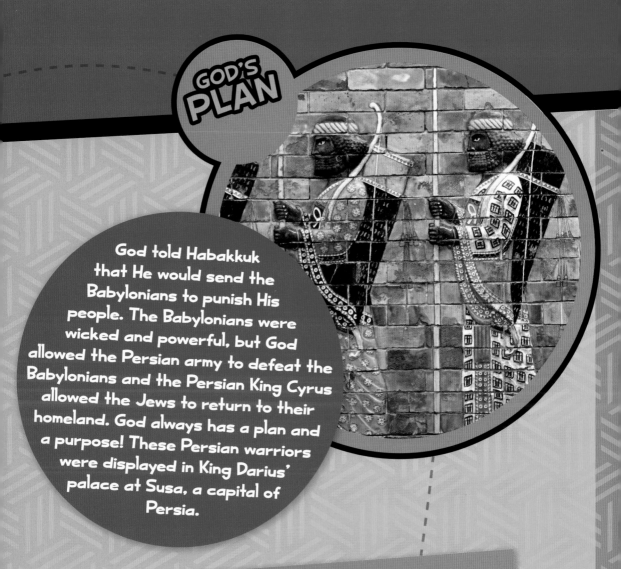

GOD'S PLAN

God told Habakkuk that He would send the Babylonians to punish His people. The Babylonians were wicked and powerful, but God allowed the Persian army to defeat the Babylonians and the Persian King Cyrus allowed the Jews to return to their homeland. God always has a plan and a purpose! These Persian warriors were displayed in King Darius' palace at Susa, a capital of Persia.

PRAYER

We can be grateful to the Lord for allowing us to know that He is righteous and sovereign. You can ask Him to help you remember to trust Him in times of confusion. You can also ask Him to help you recognize things that He is doing, and you can ask Him to give you confidence to trust Him when you do not. You can thank God for always being in control.

ZEPHANIAH
THE WARNING TO JUDAH IS TO US TOO

TEXT TRUTH

God will judge sin, but He is willing to rescue those who have faith in Him.

EXAMINE THE TEXT

ZEPHANIAH 3:17

There is a very special message in the book of Zephaniah. It is not a unique message because it is repeated in different ways throughout the Bible, but it is still very special. Zephaniah warned the people of Judah to turn to God before they faced judgment for their sin. Any time God offered a warning in the Bible, it was to offer an opportunity for repentance. Any people who were repentant and worshiped God were rescued. It is a consistent message throughout the Bible because it is what God wants us to understand. That warning from Zephaniah was not just to the people of Judah. It was a warning to us as well. So the book of Zephaniah shows us judgment and salvation.

God will judge sin. He will judge every sin committed by every person.

MEMORY VERSE

ZEPHANIAH 3:17
The LORD your God is among you, a warrior who saves. He will rejoice over you with gladness. He will be quiet in his love. He will delight in you with singing.

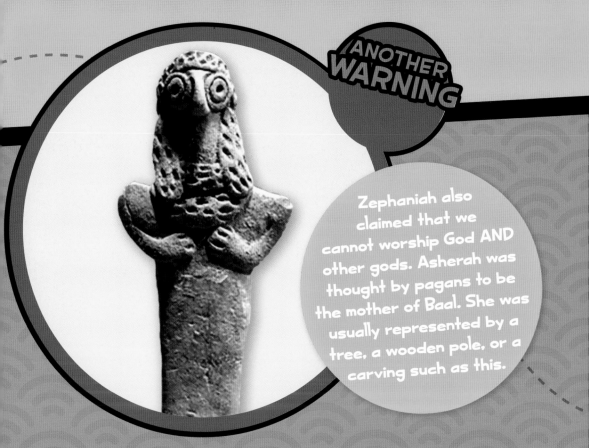

Zephaniah also claimed that we cannot worship God AND other gods. Asherah was thought by pagans to be the mother of Baal. She was usually represented by a tree, a wooden pole, or a carving such as this.

He is perfect, and all sin is an offense to Him. His justice will require every sin to be accounted for. Wow! That is serious. It is scary to think of God being angry about sin. We avoid that thought because it can make us uncomfortable. Thankfully, that is only part of the message God wants us to know.

We have to remember that God is right to punish sin. He is not being mean or cruel or unfair when He punishes sin. He is being just. God's judgment is exactly right. No one can claim that they do not deserve judgment because we are all sinners. So all of those warnings in the Bible telling people that judgment is coming are actually kind. God is being patient and generous to give people time to repent. God has given us all the examples from Scripture to show us that we have an opportunity to repent. We can pay attention to His warnings and turn away from sin.

The second part of this message is a lot more enjoyable. It is the salvation part! God has the authority to rescue sinners from judgment. That is right. Even though everyone deserves punishment for sin, He has provided a way for our sins to be forgiven. Jesus did not sin, and He died on a cross to pay the penalty of sin for others.

ZEPHANIAH

Zephaniah warned Judah, but we should all pay attention (Zephaniah 3:1).

KEY POINTS

God will judge sin (Zephaniah 3:8).

We can trust God for salvation (Zephaniah 3:17).

Because the penalty has been paid, God offers grace to forgive. He wants us to repent and have faith in Him. That is why He warns of judgment, because it helps us understand His grace.

Zephaniah 3:17 shows that God is very happy to be able to protect His people. God is happy to save sinners from His own judgment! He does not enjoy punishing sinners. He wants to rescue people from punishment. When you think of what you have learned about God's judgment and salvation through the lessons of the Israelites, you can see that His warning of judgment is part of His love for people. He wants people to turn from sin and trust Him. You can trust Him to save you.

PRAYER

We can be grateful to God for what we can learn from Zephaniah's warning and ask Him to help us understand His judgment and His gift of salvation. You can talk to God about your relationship with Him and ask Him to give you the faith you need to trust Him for salvation. You can thank Him for His grace and ask Him to help you repent and live for Him.

HAGGAI

PRIORITIES

EXAMINE THE TEXT

HAGGAI 1:5

Have you ever made a big mess with games or toys or other fun things that you had to clean up afterward?

MEMORY VERSE

HAGGAI 1:5
Now, the LORD of Armies says this: "Think carefully about your ways."

Maybe you started cleaning but got distracted by something fun and did not finish that day. Maybe it did not get finished the next day either. That is similar to what happened with the Israelites after they returned to Jerusalem from Babylon. They had been there for seventy years, so there was a lot of excitement when they returned, but they had a big mess to clean up. God had allowed Jerusalem to be destroyed as part of His judgment. When the people returned, they had no homes or walls or place to worship God. They got to work right away on restoring the temple. However, they got distracted. They started building homes and enjoying life, so the temple did not get finished. The people lived in Jerusalem for many years while the temple was left incomplete. So God sent Haggai to remind them that they needed to finish cleaning up.

Haggai helped the people understand that they were sinning by leaving the temple in ruins. They were

HAGGAI

KEY POINTS

God should be our highest priority (Haggai 1:13).

We should not allow anything to distract us from God (Haggai 1:5).

There is nothing more important than God (Haggai 1:8).

so focused on their new homes and being back in Jerusalem that they had forgotten about God. Haggai explained that there were no blessings from God because they had not made Him a priority. He mentioned that they never had enough things like food or money because they only wanted things for themselves. They did not make any effort to acquire things to rebuild the temple. The people listened to Haggai. They remembered that God deserved to be worshiped. They repented and began rebuilding the temple. Because they turned back to God, He promised to bless them.

It is easy to get distracted from following God. We have so many things that we enjoy or that we have to do each day. There can be many reasons to focus on things other than God. The people in Jerusalem had what they thought were good reasons for not finishing the temple. They needed houses; they needed resources. Their enemies were causing resistance. They had real problems that needed to be solved, but none of

those things were more important than worshiping God.

We might have many distractions in our lives too, but none are more important than God. Haggai 1:5 is a reminder to evaluate our lives. We need to pay attention to what we do and make sure we are living for God. You will probably never need to rebuild a temple for God, but He does want you to pray and obey what you learn from the Bible. Those are things we can all do to make sure that God is the highest priority in our lives. When we think of things that God wants us to do for Him, we should not wait and risk getting distracted again!

PRAYER

The Israelites did not keep God as their highest priority. We can learn from their mistake and always focus on God. You can ask God to help you live for Him regardless of the distractions in your life. You can thank God for the book of Haggai and ask Him to help you always prioritize His Word and obey what you learn. If God has not been your priority, you can ask Him to forgive you.

Solomon's Temple, which was destroyed in 586 BC by the Babylonians, had beautiful doors and pillars made of bronze and marble.

THE TEMPLE

ZECHARIAH
HOPE FOR THE FUTURE

TEXT TRUTH

We can look forward to what God has planned for the future because of Jesus.

EXAMINE THE TEXT

ZECHARIAH 10:12

You might remember that the prophet Haggai was sent to encourage the people in Jerusalem to continue rebuilding the temple. It was after their return from Babylon, and they had been distracted from God. Haggai helped them remember that God was to be their highest priority. That was an important time for the Israelites because Haggai was not the only prophet with them. Zechariah was sent to give them a message as well. Although Zechariah also encouraged them to rebuild the temple and focus on God, he had some other things to share with them. Zechariah had several visions.

The following are the visions he had and what they meant:

1. A man on a horse: God is committed to His covenant, and there is a future for His people

2. Four horns: power, specifically power over nations that resist God

3. A man with a measuring line: God would provide protection and provision

4. Joshua, the high priest: cleansing and restoration

5. Golden lampstand and two olive trees: God's infinite power and presence

MEMORY VERSE

ZECHARIAH 10:12
I will strengthen them in the LORD, and they will march in his name— this is the LORD's declaration.

6. Flying scroll: judgment for disobeying God's law

7. Woman in a basket: removal of sin

8. Four chariots: the Lord's deliverance

All of those show very important things about God and His plan, but there is more. Zechariah described someone who would not arrive for hundreds of years. He described Jesus! There were specific descriptions—such as the king who brings salvation riding a donkey—that would be seen in Jerusalem well into the future. There were also things that we have not yet seen.

All of Zechariah's messages were helpful for the Israelites to understand repentance and faith. They were also helpful to understand things to come. Zechariah challenged the people to fully dedicate themselves to God. That is the message we can learn from this too.

One of the visions that Zechariah was given from God was that of a golden lampstand and two olive trees, to show God's infinite power and presence.

ZECHARIAH

KEY POINTS

Zechariah's visions help us see God's plan (Zechariah 10:12).

More of God's plan is coming (Zechariah 12:10).

We can look forward to the future because of Jesus (Zechariah 9:9).

Zechariah's visions were not only for the people at the time, they are also for us. Zechariah 10:12 tells us that God will strengthen us as we live for Him. He wants us completely devoted, without distractions. When we commit to God, we can be ready for whatever happens. God will complete His judgment and His restoration. He will save those who have repentant faith. He will destroy sin and show His power.

God's plan is still being fulfilled. There is still time to know Him and live for Him. There are many things left for us to see from God, but we can know what to expect. God has given us His plan through the prophets, the examples of others, and most importantly, the life of Jesus. The hope we can have in Christ is more than an interesting story. It is our hope for eternity. We can learn from Zechariah's message. We can live for God, make Him our highest priority, and look forward to the future because of Jesus.

PRAYER

The book of Zechariah can help us remember that God has plans that He is still fulfilling. We can thank God for including us in His plans. You can ask God to show you ways that you can live for Him and for guidance to live out the plan He has for your life. God gives us future hope through Jesus. You can ask Him to help you to trust Him with the future and with salvation.

MALACHI

GOD WILL PUNISH, GOD WILL FORGIVE

TEXT TRUTH

God's judgment is for those who rebel against Him; His forgiveness is for those who have faith.

MEMORY VERSE

MALACHI 3:17
"They will be mine," says the LORD of Armies, "my own possession on the day I am preparing. I will have compassion on them as a man has compassion on his son who serves him."

EXAMINE THE TEXT

MALACHI 3:16-18

Malachi is the very last book in the Old Testament, which means the message in the book of Malachi is the last prophecy given before Jesus arrived. After God gave this message, He stayed silent for more than four hundred years!

Malachi was sent to Jerusalem to tell people of God's judgment. The Israelites were no longer in exile in Babylon. They were home in Jerusalem, and the temple and city walls had been rebuilt. Things should have been going well, but they were not. The people were expecting God to bless them, but no blessings were coming.

God sent Malachi to help them understand the problem.

The people might have recognized the problem if they had been paying attention to their history. They were following formal rituals without being devoted to God. They lived however they wanted and expected their burnt offerings and sacrifices to be enough

MALACHI

Do not take God's forgiveness for granted (Malachi 3:16).

KEY POINTS

God will judge sinners, but He offers forgiveness through Jesus (Malachi 3:17-18).

to satisfy God. They completely misunderstood what God wanted from them.

Malachi pointed out that the priests were distorting the truth. They could not be trusted to explain God's law, and they were not even offering the best animals to God. The people offered stolen, injured, and ill animals. God deserves our best, but they were not giving Him their best in any way.

The Israelites took God's forgiveness for granted. Their sins were as bad as they had ever been before. That is bad, especially when you think of the history of judgments they had faced because of their sins: They were rescued from Egypt but were sentenced to wander in the wilderness for forty years. They were subjected to evil kings and defeated by their enemies multiple times. The kingdom was divided. They were turned over to the Babylonians. They should have learned from all their previous mistakes. Instead, every generation repeated the same pattern of sin.

Thankfully, God is patient and forgiving. The warnings that God gives people are always opportunities to repent. That was the purpose for Malachi's message. He warned that judgment was coming. This time the judgment was not going to come in the form of exile or defeat by their enemies. This judgment would be final and eternal. That is a very serious and terrible message. We have to pay attention to this warning, because the judgment has not yet been delivered. That is why it is so important to know that God's warning comes with hope.

There is a way to escape the judgment for sin. The answer is Jesus! God offers grace through faith in Jesus. His sacrifice on the cross paid the penalty for sin. Jesus offers hope! There is forgiveness through Him. Malachi 3:16–18 shows that God will treasure those who turn to Him for salvation.

Like the Israelites, we repeat sins and take God for granted. We pay more attention to the things we like than to the things God deserves. We are guilty of sin too. That is why this message is so important for us. We need Jesus.

PRAYER

Malachi's warning to the Israelites is important for us too. We know that God's judgment can only be satisfied by Jesus, and we can thank God for sending Jesus to provide the way to be saved. You can ask the Lord to help you have faith in Jesus. You can ask Him to help you repent and trust in Jesus so that you will have no reason to fear His judgment. You can also ask Him to help you live for Him and never take His forgiveness for granted.

REFINING FIRE

To refine means to make pure or absolutely clean. In metals, heat separates the waste materials from the pure metal. This heat comes from a very, very hot fire that burns off anything unwanted from the metal. Malachi 3 says that God would send someone to refine His people, starting with the priests (Levites) and temple worship, and restore the people to Him.

1 JOHN

THE SAVED OBEY GOD

EXAMINE THE TEXT

1 JOHN 2:3-6

The book of 1 John is one of the great places in the Bible that can offer help if you have ever wondered how you can be confident that you are saved. Some people never question their salvation, but others worry that they are missing something that will prove they are saved. This book was written to assist people who were being confused by false teachings. There were people who were doubting Jesus' identity and ability to save sinners. The apostle John wrote this book to help Christians recognize what is true about Jesus and what it will look like when someone is saved.

There are three questions we should ask ourselves: *Who is Jesus? Do I have faith in Him? Do I follow His example?* The answers to the first two questions will determine whether a person is saved. The answer to the third question will provide proof of salvation.

To be sure of your salvation, you need to understand who Jesus is. He is God. He has the authority to forgive sin. He came to earth and lived His entire life without ever committing one single sin. He died on a cross to pay for sin, and those who have faith in Him will be forgiven. Knowing Jesus and having faith that His sacrifice paid the penalty for sin are the most important parts of salvation.

We sometimes think that salvation is about us, but it is actually about God. Sin is an offense against Him. Repentance is obedience to Him. Grace is a gift from Him. We can have the benefit of salvation, but we cannot do anything to earn it. It is all up to God. We are simply commanded to have faith. Those who have faith in Jesus can look to the Bible to recognize true salvation. First John 2:3–6 tells us that those who are truly saved are going to obey God. If you have faith in God and obey His Word, you have proof of your salvation. It is that simple.

When we trust God for salvation, the Holy Spirit gives us a desire to live for God. That does not mean we will always be perfect. We will sometimes have to repent and remind ourselves of the things we know about God, but He will help us with that too.

1 John tells us to "walk in the light as he himself is in the light" (verse 1:7). In ancient times, an oil lamp was kept burning because it was very hard to light and homes didn't have any other source of light at night. People replaced the oil every 2-4 hours so the lamp would stay burning.

1 JOHN

KEY POINTS

Jesus is God
(1 John 2:1).

We can trust
Jesus for
salvation
(1 John 2:1-2).

Those who
are saved will
obey God
(1 John 2:5).

God does not want us to wonder about our salvation, so He has given us verses like these to help us know what it looks like. We just have to be careful not to put too much emphasis on obedience and forget that salvation is in God's hands. We can be confident in God, even when we are not confident in our own obedience. It is good to examine what we are doing for God but better to know what God has done for us.

PRAYER

We can thank God for giving us the book of 1 John to help us understand what is true about Jesus and what it looks like to live for Him. You can ask God to help you trust Jesus for salvation and for understanding and assurance. You can ask God to give you genuine faith and to help you obey Him so that you can have confidence about your relationship with Him.

2 JOHN

TRUTH AND LOVE

TEXT TRUTH

Unity in faith, Christian fellowship, and genuine love for others always depend on truth.

EXAMINE THE TEXT

2 JOHN 1:3-6

At the time that the letter of 2 John was written, people were confusing the church with false messages about Jesus. Some of the people involved were taking advantage of people's hospitality. The people were conflicted at first because Christians are supposed to be hospitable. They thought it was the right thing to do, but the people taking advantage of them were using those opportunities to corrupt the church. John warned that the Christians should be careful not to allow such corruptions. He told them that it was good to avoid the situations that were leaving them vulnerable.

MEMORY VERSE

2 JOHN 1:6
This is love: that we walk according to his commands. This is the command as you have heard it from the beginning: that you walk in love.

When you read 2 John 1:3–6, you will see that there are two very important words in these verses: love and truth. Essentially, John was making the point that genuine Christian fellowship includes truth and love. People cannot join others

2 JOHN

Kind acts are sin if they are based on lies (2 John 1:10-11).

KEY POINTS

Genuine love and fellowship include truth (2 John 1:4-5).

Know truth so you can identify lies (2 John 1:8).

in unity with Christ if there are false teachings between them. That is because faith in Jesus is what unites Christians with other Christians.

When John wrote this letter, he wanted to help people realize that it was more important to stay true to God's Word than to be hospitable and allow corrupt teachers to spread their false messages. He wanted the people to understand that if they went along with those false teachings, they were agreeing with lies. They were not doing what was best. Instead, they were helping to spread lies about Jesus. Whether it happens through a genuine friendship or a false teacher with bad intentions, we will all encounter people who do not know God's truth. We have to remember that it is not more loving to go along with what they believe. It is more loving to commit to the truth.

The Bible is the source of truth. What you learn about God from the Bible is true. Everything you need to know about Jesus is in the Bible. He is God. He died on the cross to pay

for sin. He fulfilled God's Law. He is returning someday. Everything we can know about Jesus and how to live for Him is available for us to know. The Bible has all the truth we need, and if you study the Bible, you will be able to avoid the mistakes of those John wrote to. You will become able to identify if something is false, and you will not be tempted to go along with a lie.

SPEAK TRUTH

The Romans built amphitheaters where people would speak to the public. Although some people made up lies about Jesus, John wrote about the importance of speaking the truth. We can know if someone speaks truth by knowing the Bible.

PRAYER

We can thank God for giving us examples to learn from in the Bible and for making a way for us to understand the importance of truth in our lives. You can ask Him to help you know what is true. You can ask Him to help you obey Him, know how to be an example to others who do not know truth, and keep you from being confused by false beliefs.

3 JOHN

BE SUPPORTIVE

TEXT TRUTH

One of the ways we can be obedient to God's Word is to support those who teach the Bible.

EXAMINE THE TEXT

3 JOHN 1:8

You probably remember that in the book of 2 John a church was being corrupted by false teachings, and John warned the Christians to be careful not to support those who were introducing the lies. He recommended that they not show them hospitality. That just meant that they should not give them opportunities to corrupt the church, and they should not give them help as they spread their false messages. In the book of 3 John there is a different problem with hospitality. Christians were not supporting those who were traveling through to spread God's message. This was a problem because if someone traveled from far away in those days, there were not many options for places to stay or get food. They depended on the people living in the area to help them.

Third John 1:8 shows that Christian people should have been showing hospitality and giving support to the traveling ministers. The book of 3 John was written to celebrate a man named Gaius for supporting them exactly as he should. John said that Gaius was being obedient to God's Word. He called it "walking in truth."

Any time you obey the Bible you are walking in truth or living according to God's Word. You might not have an opportunity to follow Gaius's example

MEMORY VERSE

3 JOHN 1:8

We ought to support such people so that we can be coworkers with the truth.

in exactly the same way, but you can support those who preach the Word of God. Whether they are preachers, missionaries, Bible study leaders, or parents, there are ways to support the people you know who teach the Bible and tell people about Jesus.

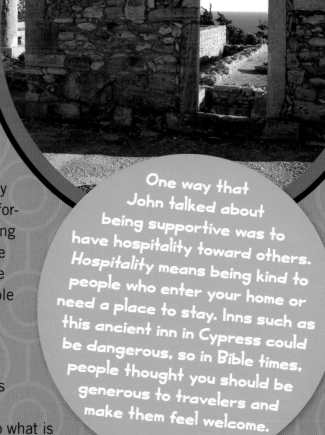

- You can pray. When people teach the Bible, they have an extra responsibility. They are not just teaching information. They are teaching how to know God and be saved from sin. They are teaching truths for people to live by. Prayer is a powerful way to support others.

- You can give. Sometimes people need money or supplies to be able to do what is necessary to teach people the Bible.

One way that John talked about being supportive was to have hospitality toward others. Hospitality means being kind to people who enter your home or need a place to stay. Inns such as this ancient inn in Cypress could be dangerous, so in Bible times, people thought you should be generous to travelers and make them feel welcome.

3 JOHN

We should be obedient to God's Word (3 John 1:4).

Gaius is an example of someone who walked in truth (3 John 1:3).

We can learn from Gaius and support those who teach God's Word (3 John 1:8).

Of course, while you are a kid, you might not have as many opportunities to give money or resources, but you can give when you are able.

- You can serve. Everyone needs help. You might be able to do things like carry supplies, pass out papers, hold a door open, or offer a drink of water. There are always opportunities to serve in small ways that can be a big help.

- You can encourage. Not everyone will be eager to hear what is being taught from the Bible. They might complain or argue. Sometimes even those who agree might not say anything. It is always nice for someone to be encouraged.

- You can listen. There are always distractions when someone is talking about the Bible. Paying attention is a great way to be supportive.

There are many ways to support those who teach the Word of God. We can take advantage of the opportunities God gives us to show Christian hospitality in that way. We will be obedient to God and an encouragement to others at the same time. Plus, it will be fun!

PRAYER

You can thank God for Gaius's example of hospitality and obedience. Ask God to help you follow Gaius's example and be an example to others. You can ask God to show you opportunities to support those who teach the Bible. You can also ask Him to help you serve others with the right attitude and out of obedience to Him.

REVELATION
THE FINAL MESSAGE

TEXT TRUTH

Sin has a permanent consequence, but Jesus provided the permanent solution on the cross.

The book of Revelation is filled with information about Jesus and salvation. It warns people of God's judgment of sin so they can repent. Revelation explains that Jesus will return for His people and will eliminate sin from the world. It also describes a new earth that will be made perfect when sin is removed.

EXAMINE THE TEXT

REVELATION 5; 14:6

There is no book in the Bible more complicated to understand than the book of Revelation. It can be confusing, but do not worry. God did not give us a book in the Bible to confuse us. He has an important message for us in Revelation, and you can understand it. Sure, some of the unusual symbols will require a lot of study, and many people disagree about what they mean. If you can keep from getting distracted by all the things you do not understand in this book, you will be surprised by everything you can understand.

MEMORY VERSE

REVELATION 14:6

I saw another angel flying high overhead, with the eternal gospel to announce to the inhabitants of the earth—to every nation, tribe, language, and people.

REVELATION

KEY POINTS

There is a permanent consequence for sin and a permanent solution for sin (Revelation 5:4-5).

Jesus will return someday to rescue people who have trusted in Him. (Revelation 6:16-17; 7:10).

These things are all just the conclusion to the rest of the Bible. They tell us that an end will come. God's warning of judgment will not be like the warnings of the past. There will be no defeats by foreign armies or exiles. It will be a permanent consequence for sin. Thankfully, as always, there is hope through Jesus. When you read through Revelation 5, you will see that Jesus is the only one worthy to open the scroll, the Lamb that was slain, and the one who was worshiped. His sinless life made it possible for Him to be the perfect sacrifice to pay for the sins of others. By trusting in Him, we can be forgiven of sin and have eternal life with God.

Over and over again in the Bible God warns us of the consequence of sin, which helps us recognize and appreciate the gift of salvation. It is God's generous way of offering an opportunity to repent and trust in Jesus. Revelation is that final message.

If you think of all the people you know, you will probably think of some who do not understand God's message.

They might not know that sin has consequences and Jesus made a way to be forgiven. There are many people in the world who do not know Jesus, but there is still time to tell them.

Revelation 14:6 tells us that God's message is intended for everyone. He will put people in your life whom He wants you to tell about repentance and forgiveness through Jesus. He might ask you to go to another country someday to meet people, or He might want you to tell a friend you already know right now. You can share the message of the Bible with others so they can have faith in Jesus and live for Him.

PRAYER

The things that you do for God while you are on this earth will last forever. You can talk to God about what He wants you to do for Him. You can thank God for giving us the Bible so that we can know Him and know how to live for Him. You can also ask the Lord to help you keep eternity in mind and live in a way that helps others know about His love and willingness to forgive sinful people.

Most ancient writings were only written on one side of a document because it was difficult to write on the back of papyrus and leather. John described a scroll written on both sides and sealed with seven seals, like the way a Roman will was made in the first century. The seals were opened when the owner of the will died. Only one person was worthy to open the seals in the book of Revelation—the Lamb of God!

BIBLE SKILLS

LOCATE BOOKS AND PASSAGES IN THE BIBLE

If you want to run in a race, you have to train, especially if you want to win! The way to get faster at something is to practice. There is a skill that every person should practice that will help while reading God's Word. This skill is finding the books of the Bible. There are several different ways to practice this skill.

1. For this activity, begin by writing each of the sixty-six books of the Bible on individual notecards. Mix up the notecards and randomly select one, then find the book in the Bible that corresponds to whichever card you picked. You might need to begin by searching the table of contents. However, do not rely on that too much. Once you have gotten better at finding the books, challenge yourself to find them faster. Continue to practice every day for a while until you can find any book right away.

2. Turn to the table of contents. It will probably be located on one of the first few pages of your Bible. This will list all the books of the Bible in order. Randomly select a book from the list, and open your Bible to where you think it will be located. If you are not correct, refer to the table of contents to see whether you should turn forward or backward to find your book. Repeat this

until you are able to find at least one book without looking back at the list.

3. Open your Bible to the book of Psalms. If you have never searched for chapters and verses within a book of the Bible, look for the numbers. The larger numbers are marking the chapters, and the smaller numbers are marking the verses. Now find and read the following verses: Psalm 19:1, 118:24, 119:105, 145:9, and 150:6. Remember, the first number is the chapter, and the second is the verse.

4. It is important that we know how to find the specific things we learn in the Bible. The following list is what you will use for this game:
   • Naomi's Moabite daughter-in-law stayed with her (Ruth 1).
   • David became king (2 Samuel 5).
   • Paul confronted Peter for hypocrisy (Galatians 2).
   • Jesus healed the man with the withered hand (Mark 3).
   • God sent a message to Nineveh (Jonah 3).
   • Jesus corrected the disciples for arguing about who will be greater (Luke 22).
   • Only Caleb and Joshua were allowed into the promised land (Numbers 26).
   • A servant of God was tested and still trusted that the Redeemer lives (Job 19).
   • God asked who would go and His servant said, "Send me" (Isaiah 6).

- Elijah challenged the people on Mount Carmel to only worship the one true God (1 Kings 18).

Write each of those statements on individual notecards without including the Bible reference. Mix them up, and randomly select one. Try to remember where the selected story is found in the Bible. Turn to that book and see if you are correct. Make three attempts before checking the answer. This will be a difficult challenge, but be sure to have a lot of fun!

KNOW THE BOOKS AND DIVISIONS OF THE BIBLE

1. Place sixty-six sticky notes on the floor. Make sure you can step or hop from one sticky note to the next. You can be creative in how you place the sticky notes. For example, one piece might be very close or very far away from the next piece. Write the books of the Bible in order on the sticky notes. Write the words very small so that you can't see the writing too well. That way you have help if you need it but won't rely on it. Step on the first sticky note and say the first book of the Bible. Go to the second one and do the same. Repeat with every sticky note until you have said all the books in the Bible. Keep practicing and notice how much faster you get each time.

2. If you are learning the books of the Bible, this will be a fun way to practice which books belong in the Old Testament and which books belong in the New Testament. Get two paper bags. Write "Old Testament" on the front of one and "New Testament" on the front of the other. Place them near each other on the floor. Write the names of each of the books of the Bible on individual pieces of paper. Crumple the papers into balls and mix them up. Stand several feet away from the paper bags. Select a ball, and say the name of the book written on it. Then toss the ball into the correct bag for where the book can be found in the Bible. Repeat with each ball. If you are not sure which bag it belongs in, look in the Bible to find out before tossing it.

3. Did you know that there are divisions in the Bible that group books into specific categories based on each type of writing? It is helpful to know the divisions, because they show us important things about the way each book of the Bible was originally meant to be read. That helps us understand the books better. There are ten divisions, with five for the Old Testament and five for the New Testament. The Old Testament divisions are Law, History, Poetry and Wisdom, Major Prophets, and Minor Prophets. The New Testament divisions are Gospels, History, Paul's Letters, General Letters, and Prophecy.

To practice the divisions, write each book of the Bible on an individual notecard. Get ten sheets of paper and write one division on each piece.

Place the papers around the room. Randomly select a notecard, and put it with the appropriate paper for whatever division it belongs in. Repeat until you are confident that you know which books belong in each division.

4. For this activity, you will make your own bookmarks. These will not just be decorative bookmarks. They will also help you remember the divisions of the Bible. Cut enough paper to make ten bookmarks. Once the bookmarks are cut, write the books of each division on separate bookmarks. You can place these in your Bible to help you practice the divisions of the Bible.

5. For this activity you will need a small box, a marker, and notecards. On each side of the box, write one of the following phrases: *before and after, division, find it, pronounce it, Old or New,* and *say a verse.* On individual notecards, write the books of the

Bible. Mix the cards, and select one randomly. Roll the box. Do whichever phrase lands facing up.

- If it lands on *before and after*, say the books of the Bible that come before and after the one selected.
- If it lands on *division*, say the division of the Bible the selected book is in.
- If it lands on *find it,* open your Bible to the selected book.
- If it lands on *pronounce it*, say the book out loud. Get help if you do not know how to pronounce it.
- If it lands on *Old or New,* say whether the selected book is in the Old or New Testament.
- If it lands on *say a verse*, either find a verse in that book to read or recite one from memory.

This activity will help you learn the books of the Bible better and practice verses. Be sure to have fun!

USE RESOURCES

Every story in the Bible is part of a bigger story. In many Bibles there are extra notes and resources to help us understand how to use the Bible and how it is organized. Each book of the Bible will have an outline summarizing the key points. You might need to borrow a Bible if yours does not include outlines.

Open your Bible to the book of 1 Samuel. On one of the pages before the book begins you should find the outline for 1 Samuel. It will emphasize important points from the book and give a general idea about what is included. Search the outline to find a reference to chapter 8 where the people of Israel demand a king. Although that chapter is a full story, it is only part of a much bigger story. Look at all the important moments documented in the outline. Consider how one chapter fits in the entire book of 1 Samuel and how the book of 1 Samuel fits in the entire Bible.

You can do this with other books and chapters in the Bible too!

SHARE THE BIBLE

If you had an opportunity, would you know how to tell someone the message of Jesus? What would be the most important things to explain? When it comes to the message of Jesus, we want to be able to tell people about Him whenever we have a chance. It is a good idea to practice what you might say to someone. You can look for verses that help you and plan the most important points you want to make. If you practice finding the specific verses you want you use, you will always be able to show someone else when you get the opportunity.

1. Open your Bible, and read Romans 3:23–24. These verses tell us that we have all sinned, which means we all need forgiveness. People are forgiven by God's grace through Jesus' sacrifice on the cross. Read Ephesians 2:8–10. This shows that salvation is from God, and there is nothing we can do to earn it. We are saved by grace through faith. Good works do not earn salvation; they result from salvation. Do those verses seem helpful?

   If you want to talk about salvation with someone, you can show them these verses. You can tell them other things you know from the Bible too.

2. Whether we are familiar with certain Bible verses or we are just learning, we should always look carefully at a verse and consider what it means. Open your Bible and read Genesis 1:1. What does that verse tell you? Did you notice that it identifies the power and authority of

God? After all, He created everything. Consider all the things you can know and tell others from that verse.

Read John 3:16. What does that verse tell you? How would you explain that to someone? That verse helps us understand God's love and salvation through faith in Jesus.

Read Luke 6:31. What does that verse tell you? This is a great verse to help us remember how to treat people.

Read 1 Timothy 4:12. What does that verse tell you? Do you think you could explain that verse to someone? You could tell them that it is an encouragement for us to be good Christian examples.

Read those verses again, and practice explaining them to someone. This will help you learn them better, but it will also prepare you for whenever you have a real opportunity to explain them to others.

3. A fun way to remember the details of a particular Bible story is to draw a picture of it. This will also give you a way to describe it to someone else. If you do not already have a particular passage in mind, consider reading one of the following stories:
   - Daniel 6:16–23 (God protected Daniel in the lions' den.)
   - Luke 19:1–10 (Zacchaeus climbed a tree to see Jesus.)
   - Genesis 7:6–10 (Noah and the animals entered the ark.)

   Make sure to follow what the Bible says, not what you remember about the story. It will help you pay attention to the details in the Bible. Any time you want to remember something from the Bible, drawing a picture is a good way to help! Practice using the picture to explain what the story tells us about God and how to live for Him. You should read more verses before and after each story if you want more context.

READ THE BIBLE

The most important book ever written is the Bible. It is important to read the Bible every day so we can learn more and more about God. The more we read the Bible, the better we know Him. If you are not used to reading the Bible every day, you might need some type of reminder. There are several different ways to remind yourself to read the Bible.

1. One great way is to make your own calendar. If you do not have a blank calendar to use, get some colored paper and draw squares to represent each day. In each square, write a specific reference to a verse or passage that you plan to read. You can choose memory verses, verses from a specific book in the Bible, or any other plan. You get to decide how many verses you read each day. After you have the references written on the calendar, you can decorate it. Once your calendar is complete, display it in a place where you will notice it every day. It will help you remember to read your Bible so you can learn more of God's truth each day.

2. Make a reminder that you can display to help you commit to read the Bible every day. It can be something that hangs on your wall or mirror or even on the front of a notebook, but it needs to be something that you see often and that gets your attention when you see it.

One idea is to make a door hanger. This is simply a piece of cardboard or thick paper with a hole cut in it to fit over the doorknob. Write "READ THE BIBLE" in large letters on the front of the door hanger, then decorate the it. When you hang it on your doorknob, you will be reminded every day to read the Bible. Pray that God will help you commit to your daily reading plan.

APPLY BIBLE LESSONS

1. Open your Bible, and read Philippians 4:4. That verse tells us to rejoice in the Lord. To obey God in this way requires a plan. Get out a piece of paper and a pen. Write the following sentences on your paper
   - Thank You, God, for giving me _____.
   - Thank You, God, for helping me _____.
   - Thank You, God, for showing me _____.
   - I am happy today that _____.

   Now that you have these sentences, you have a plan to rejoice! At the end of each day you can look at the paper and fill in the blanks based on whatever God is doing in your life. For example, one day you might be grateful that He showed you a specific verse in the Bible.

   By the way, this can also be helpful when you pray and when you talk to your family about the day. However you decide to use this, it can remind you of God's Word and how to rejoice in Him.

2. A lot of times we compare ourselves to others. We compare ourselves to our friends, our classmates, our family members, and so on. It is not necessarily sinful to be like others, but there is someone that the Bible tells us to always strive to be more like: Jesus. Open your Bible, and find the following verses to see exactly what God wants:
   - 1 John 2:6
   - 1 Corinthians 11:1
   - Galatians 2:20
   - Ephesians 2:10

   What are some ways that you can be like Jesus today? Make a list of ways that you know you can be like Jesus. Write the ways from your list on individual craft sticks. Place the craft sticks in a cup. Make sure you cannot see what is written on the craft sticks, and randomly select one.

   Whichever craft stick you select will be your challenge for the day. Spend the rest of the day trying to do whatever is written. Remember that it is a way to be like Jesus, so take it seriously, but have fun! Challenge yourself to select a new stick every day.

MEMORIZE PASSAGES

Write the references to the memory verses from this book on individual notecards. The reference is the book, chapter, and verse number. It will look like this: *Proverbs 2:6*. Mix the cards up, and select one randomly. Recite the verse referenced on the card. If you do not know the verse, look it up in the Bible. Read it until you are able to recite it. Continue selecting cards and practicing verses until you are confident with all of the memory verses.

REMEMBER:

All Scripture is inspired by God and is profitable for teaching, for rebuking, for correcting, for training in righteousness, so that the man of God may be complete, equipped for every good work.—2 Timothy 3:16–17

READ:

Read Psalm 119:11. The psalmist declares that he has "treasured" or "hidden" (NIV) God's Word in his heart so that he can keep from sinning. Sometimes it can be difficult to know if something is a sin. Parents and teachers can help guide us, but the best source for learning right and wrong, and what makes something a sin, is the Bible—God's Word. If we don't study God's Word—read it, understand it, remember it—then we are ultimately relying on the opinions of others to determine what is acceptable. We can't be sure to do what is right in God's eyes unless we know what He says is right. So spend some time with your Bible, and if you need help to understand what it means, ask an adult you can trust. Once you know what your Bible says, you can use that knowledge to live the way God wants you to live. That's how you treasure God's Word.

THINK:

1. Name three things you learned about the Bible, God, or His people from this devotional.

2. Why do you think God's people had such a hard time being loyal and obedient to God?

3. Why do you think people still struggle today to be loyal and obedient to God?

4. What is something that people say is right or acceptable to do but God says is wrong?

5. Who can you ask for help to understand what God's Word is telling you?

6. What is something you've learned from the Bible that is right? Something wrong?